Something Understood

Something Understood

AN ANTHOLOGY
OF POETRY AND PROSE

Introduced by
MARK TULLY

Compiled by
BEVERLEY MCAINSH

Hodder & Stoughton
LONDON SYDNEY AUCKLAND

First published in Great Britain in 2001, by arrangement with
the BBC.

This paperback edition first published in 2002

Something Understood is based on the BBC Radio 4 programme.

BBC Radio 4 word mark and logo are trademarks of the British
Broadcasting Corporation and are used under licence.
BBC logo copyright © 1996.

British Library Cataloguing in Publication Data
A record for this book is available from the British Library

ISBN 0 340 86124 X

Typeset in Monotype Fournier by
Strathmore Publishing Services, London N7

Printed and bound in Great Britain by
Clays Ltd, St Ives plc

Hodder and Stoughton Ltd
A Division of Hodder Headline Ltd
338 Euston Road
London NW1 3BH

Contents

Introduction by Mark Tully

Mahatma Gandhi, one of my favourite contributors to *Something Understood*, once wrote, 'In my pursuit after Truth I have discarded many ideas and learnt many new things. Old as I am in age, I have no feeling that I have ceased to grow inwardly, or that my growth will stop with the dissolution of the flesh.' The poetry and prose I have read to prepare programmes for *Something Understood*, the different traditions of music I have listened to, the people of diverse experiences, learning and wisdom I have conversed with have led me 'to discard many ideas and learn many new things'. They have reinforced my belief that we can indeed understand some things but not all and that, though our understanding can grow, we must never sit back and say 'Now I fully understand'. Furthermore they have strengthened my conviction that whatever awaits us after death will not be an end to understanding. So perhaps the best way I can introduce this collection of poems, prose and interviews is to describe something of their meaning for me.

I was thrilled when Beverley chose to introduce the first chapter, 'They that love beyond the world: Understanding love and friendship', with an extract from an interview with my oldest friend, D'Arcy O'Farrell. D'Arcy has lived a quiet life as a hospital administrator, never seeking fame or fortune, content to be of good repute and to be the centre of the circle of friends who surrounded him at university and still surround him. He can truly be said to have the gift of friendship. Yet he made it clear that, however gifted you are, friendships need to be kept in good repair, which means taking trouble. 'You must keep in contact with people and you must make some sort of an effort. It's no use sitting around and waiting for the other fellow to come to you.' So often friendships wither and love grows cold because the initial excitement wears off and we do not persevere in deepening the relationship. It can only deepen by living through the duller moments, by arguing out the inevitable differences and overcoming the distances too, as D'Arcy suggested.

'Miraculous alchemy: Understanding the natural world' brings me to a concern no one living in India can ignore – our assault on nature. Most mornings when I'm in Delhi, Gilly and I take our dog for a walk in a garden which adjoins one of the city's finest monuments, Humayun's tomb, seen by many as the precursor of the Taj Mahal. It's not a well-tended garden – nature is left with a free hand for the most part. A peacock in all his splendour sometimes stands on the dome of a medieval mosque; a young peahen and her family, less resplendent, stalk through the long grass; green pigeons, rather late risers, hunch their shoulders as squawking parakeets and brightly coloured coppersmiths attack the fruit of a peepul tree. The ground under the Harsinghar is carpeted orange and white with the flowers the tree sheds every night. Yet often the cloudless sky is a dirty polluted grey and always the roar of the traffic causing that pollution can be heard in the distance. The beauty nature has gifted to India contrasts with the ugliness we have created, an ugliness so strikingly described in the words of Gerard Manley Hopkins' poem 'God's Grandeur':

> Generations have trod, have trod, have trod;
> And all is seared with trade; bleared, smeared with toil;
> And wears man's smudge and shares man's smell …

Yet rereading the poem I was reminded that, for all the depressing evidence that we are still not serious about removing those smudges or sweetening the smell, we should not despair because 'nature is never spent; there lives the dearest freshness deep down things'. But, of course, that doesn't mean we can or indeed should leave it to nature to compensate for our greed and folly. We need a new commitment to nature, a commitment as strong as the American Indian Chief Seathl's testament.

No *Something Understood* is an island unto itself. Themes cross and recross programmes. One theme which I have found particularly meaningful is the need to be true to ourselves. That chimes in with another theme – that we should not be too hard on ourselves, we should not be obsessed by our failures and our sins. The two themes are brought together by the theologian Philip Sheldrake in the chapter 'And I to my pledged word am true: Understanding the best that we can be'. He advocates that 'we attend to our desires', for then, he maintains, 'we'll discover the directions our lives should take, and that from within rather than something imposed from outside'. The last point is surely so important in an age when we are under pressure from all sides to take the path others want us to follow – the management consultants who would have us conform to their pattern, be cogs in machines; the advertisers who hope to convince us that they know our needs better than we ourselves do; the journalists who imply celebrity status, salary or sex bring happiness. Those are not the desires Philip Sheldrake talks about. He says, 'self-fulfilment is never self-centredness'.

In the chapter 'Is this where God hides?: Understanding the quest for God', we come to questions we have discussed time and time again in *Something Understood* – where and how do we find

God? I am always excited by the evidence that so many writers, from so many different countries and cultures, faiths and traditions, some born in my lifetime, some born thousands of years ago, have found similar answers to those questions. The writers I have come across in *Something Understood* have enormously strengthened my belief that there are indeed many roads to God but they all lead to the same destination. That confirms my faith in God too. In this chapter representing the East, Sarojini Nayadu, an Indian poet and a disciple of Mahatma Gandhi, writes of the search for God,

> With futile hands we seek to gain
> Our inaccessible desire,
> Diviner summits to attain,
> With faith that sinks and feet that tire
> But nought shall conquer or control
> The heavenward hunger of our soul.

From the West, John Masefield also writes of the difficult road that hunger leads us along:

> Friends and loves we have none, nor wealth nor blessed abode,
> But the hope of the City of God at the other end of the road.

The image of life as a journey can leave us with the impression that we can only experience God at the end of that journey. In the same chapter, the Sufi Mystic Bábá Kúhí of Shíráz, in his poem 'Only God I Saw', tells another story, and Francis Thompson finds Christ 'walking on the water not of Gennesareth, but Thames'.

Moderation and balance are two more themes which run through many programmes. It was from Hinduism that I learnt life was a continuous struggle to retain our balance, the middle way between surrendering to our desires and suppressing them. From *Something Understood* I discovered that this wisdom was to be found in Christian thinkers too. I particularly like the anonymous prayer of a seventeenth-century nun in the chapter called 'I'll hold your hand: Understanding youth and age'. She warns us that we can be unbalanced in our desire to be godly. In her prayer she asks God to help her avoid all excesses including saintliness: 'Keep me reasonably sweet; I do not want to be a Saint – some of them are so hard to live with.' They are indeed. They set such unattainable examples that, if you are anything like me, you are tempted to write off the whole venture, to abandon any attempt to learn from them.

The nun desires to grow old in a balanced faith. In the same chapter there is another anonymous poem, 'The Song of an Old Woman Abandoned By Her Tribe'. It's a poignant song which all those who now undervalue age and experience should read, for it is certain that the balance, the mutual respect and support there should be between the different ages in our society has become tilted in favour of the young. The natural balance is symbolised in the poem by Margaret Cropper which has given the title to this chapter. The poem is the story of an old woman who was afraid that she would fall on some steps until she heard a childish voice and then felt 'into my hand a very small hand came, peacefully holding mine'.

The chapter 'I believe no pain is lost: Understanding consolation' introduces the difficult, delicate subject of suffering. In Christianity the cross is a symbol of good rising from the ashes of defeat and despair, from suffering. Taking this as their text, preachers sometimes tell us that suffering is necessary for salvation or, to put it more crudely, that suffering is good for us. Such teaching can be cruel to those who suffer, underestimating their pain and cheapening their sorrow. Yet in this chapter Dame Cicely Saunders, who has seen so much suffering as the pioneer of the hospice movement, says, 'We're in a world in which love and loss seem to go together and perhaps they have to.' In her own life she has found 'the hardest times have brought the best joys'. Dame Cicely believes that those who are suffering don't need explanations or exhortations but sympathy, 'the arm round the shoulder, even your own tears'.

The mystery of a loving God who allows suffering is very deep, but *Something Understood* has fortified my conviction that we cannot dismiss God because there is suffering in the world. Who could be a more valiant witness to that than Sheila Cassidy? After all that she underwent as a prisoner in Chile she could still write,

> I believe that pain
> and prayer
> are somehow saved,
> processed,
> stored,
> used in the Divine Economy.

We are often told that we live in a society which is over competitive, that success and achievement are too narrowly defined, and I wouldn't say no to that. During my days at achievement-oriented English schools I adopted the middle way. I didn't try to be top of the class – I would almost certainly have failed if I had – but I did ensure I wasn't bottom either. As I grew up I came to realise I was limiting my ambitions by fear of failure. But it wasn't until I came to read the Hindu scripture the

Bhagavad Gita that I understood the answer – we should not look for success or fear failure; we should do what we do to the best of our ability and leave the outcome to God. After all, failure is often an indication that we are not doing God's will for us. Even when we are successful we know, if we think about it, that luck, fate, call it what you will, has played a major part. If we do come top of the class it's due in no small measure to the accident of our being born with a particular type of intelligence. What we need to do is to discern the will of God for us, and in the chapter 'Good luck? Bad luck? Who knows?: Understanding hard times', an Indian Christian priest, Anthony de Mello, tells a delightful story which makes that point much better than I can.

In *Something Understood* we are always coming across apparent contradictions. How can we believe in God's will and free will at the same time; in joy arising from suffering; in an omnipotent God who allows us to smear and blear his creation; in a future after death when death itself appears to be so final? So we have a chapter titled 'God of all the opposites: Understanding tension and paradox'. At the heart of all this paradox is the apparent contradiction between reason and faith. The theologian Keith Ward, who has written extensively on science (which represents reason) and religion (which goes beyond it), bridges the contradiction between the two: 'There is no conflict between reason, the deepest understanding of the cosmos, and faith, the trusting response to the mystery of divine love. Together, they express the commitment to truth that should be the hallmark of science and the humility that should be the hallmark of faith.' When I was an undergraduate I used to fear that my belief in the existence of God would become untenable because of the discoveries of science. Because of writers like Keith Ward I am no longer so naive.

Humility is perhaps the least valued virtue today, but surely the key to so much understanding. Religion goes wrong when it claims to possess certainty, to have the one and only true report of God. In the last chapter, 'Walk out with me: Understanding the journey', the travel writer William Dalrymple suggests that all the troubles of the world come from the suppression of the urge to keep on the move, from 'being locked up in the walls of a city'. William has done a great deal of travel but for some years he did settle in Delhi and wrote a book about the city, which includes a fine description of the Muslim shrine opposite where I have lived probably far longer than he would recommend. His city walls are a vivid image of those who are walled up in their own certainty. They should think on the words of that great churchman, the Venerable Bede, who wrote about the brief life of man 'of which we know neither what goes before nor what comes after'.

The very title *Something Understood* suggests humility and acceptance of the limitations of our own powers to understand. But there goes the contradiction again, because surely we should still go on trying to understand? After all, there are many scientists who have the humility to acknowledge that the more they understand, the more they are struck by the miraculous mechanism of a universe they could never create.

Something Understood has helped me to acknowledge the limits of my understanding but there is more to it than that. I have also been greatly heartened by all those people who have escaped from reason's imprisonment, gone outside those city walls and experienced God. They, like the poet Christina Georgina Rossetti, have confidence that, no matter how uphill our journey through life may be, we cannot miss the Inn at the end and there will be beds for all who come.

Mark Tully

Preface

Something Understood is a secret shared by nearly a million people. Despite being scheduled very early and very late – at 6.05 a.m. and 11.30 p.m. every Sunday on BBC Radio 4 – that is the number of listeners the programme attracts each week, according to the BBC's own audience research.

The programme was launched in April 1995, taking its name from the last line of George Herbert's poem 'Prayer'. Each week we explore a different theme, seeking the understanding of our title through poetry and prose, music and conversation. The themes are wide-ranging – some serious, some light-hearted – but always touch on life's deeper questions and experiences, and always reflect, too, a belief in the reality of an underlying spiritual dimension to life. God is, however variously defined, a given, in *Something Understood*.

When the programme first began there was a sharp volley of complaint from those who objected to the loss of the long-running *Bells on Sunday*; but the tone of the letters soon changed dramatically. So many people wrote or called to check the title of a particular piece of music, or of a poem that had spoken to them, that we began compiling a weekly information sheet, listing the programme content. Many listeners also asked for tapes or scripts, but copyright law prevented us from being able to help with the first request, and Mark Tully's handwriting the second! Still others wrote appreciatively, and very personally, of how the programme had touched a deep chord within them, sometimes because they were experiencing hard and painful times, and sometimes quite the opposite, because the programme had voiced for them a sense of celebration, perhaps, or of gratitude, or discovery.

Radio is a uniquely powerful medium for exploring ideas and experiences: it is immediate, intimate and personal, yet at the same time it makes a community of its listeners: a community in which develops a sense of continuity and shared experience. Judging from our letters, calls and e-mails, and from many chance conversations in some very unlikely places, this is what has happened with *Something Understood*.

But there is a downside to radio, and that is its essentially ephemeral nature. We are fortunate that our programme is repeated, but at midnight each Sunday it is gone, like Cinderella's coach, for ever. A book, of course, is much more durable, and that is the reason for bringing this collection out now: to respond to the hundreds of requests we have received to translate *Something Understood* into a more lasting medium.

Something is, sadly, always lost in translation: in print there is no way of conveying the vital role of music in the programme, nor the timbre of the presenter's voice, nor the train of thought in their script, and the anecdotes and insights that enable the listener to feel they know them in some measure. But what we can do is offer an anthology which, for all that is missing, does still remain true both to the spirit and to the content of *Something Understood*.

To compile this collection, I have read back through every item we have ever used in the programme. I was intrigued to see how our hundreds of different themes fell naturally into a number of larger categories, and it is these that have provided the subjects for the ten chapters here.

As in the programme, each chapter contains a wide range of material, drawn from many centuries, continents, cultures and faiths. Some of the pieces will be familiar: Thomas Hardy's 'The Darkling Thrush', for example, and Shelley's 'Ozymandias', which, interestingly, have been the two poems which we have used most often in the last five years. But much of the writing will be less familiar, reflecting our concern to stretch our boundaries and expand our repertoire with each new programme, mining the literary and spiritual treasures of past and present alike.

To further our quest for understanding, many of our programmes contain conversations. Guests have included well-known figures like Lord Howe, Dame Cicely Saunders and Professor Richard Dawkins; they have included respected academics and prominent figures in the field of religion and spirituality; and they have included, above all, many private individuals who have shared generously of their time, wisdom and experience. In order to preserve something of this element in the programme, each chapter contains extracts from some of the conversations Mark has enjoyed over the years.

In the millennium year, 2000, Danah Zohar and Ian Marshall published a book called *Spiritual Intelligence: the Ultimate Intelligence*. The opening chapter contains the following statement:

> The full picture of human intelligence can be completed with a discussion of our spiritual intelligence – SQ for short. By SQ I mean the intelligence with which we address and solve problems of meaning and value, the intelligence with which we can place our actions and our lives in a wider, richer, meaning-giving context, the intelligence with which we can assess that one course of action or one life-path is more meaningful than another. SQ is the

necessary foundation for the effective functioning of both IQ and
EQ [emotional intelligence]. It is our ultimate intelligence.

This statement resonates powerfully for me, both personally and
in relation to *Something Understood*, illuminating as it does the
context and value of life's spiritual dimension. That is, as I have
said, the dimension that lies at the very heart of *Something
Understood*, and also, I hope, at the heart of this collection.

Beverley McAinsh

Thanks

Something Understood stands or falls on the quality of its research and we give our most heartfelt thanks to our excellent researchers: Frank Stirling and John Florance on poetry and prose, and Adrian Edwards and Keith Lankester on music.

At the other end of the production process, we thank our regular sound engineer, Tim Morgan of Intaudiom, for his skill and perfectionist tendencies, and Shane Wall and his colleagues at Unique Facilities.

We thank Mike Wooldridge, BBC Bureau Chief in Delhi, and his colleagues for their welcome and for allowing us to use their studios and other facilities. Beverley thanks Ruth Wooldridge and Gilly Wright in Delhi, and Maggie Tully in London, for their warm and generous hospitality.

Something Understood is very much a team effort: its range and freshness depend on the contributions and suggestions of many people, from our Executive Editor, Laura Parfitt, to our PA, Emma Leighton, who also managed the laborious task of copyright clearance for this book, with patience and good humour.

We thank presenters Fergal Keane, Eileen Campbell and Peter Hobday, and producer Tamsin Collison, for all they have brought to the programme.

Our readers, too, are a vital part of the success of the programme and over the years many actors have worked with us. Perhaps most regularly, Emma Fielding, Emily Raymond, Hermione Norris, Nicholas Boulton, David Holt and, again,

Frank Stirling, who have each made their own special contribution to *Something Understood*.

While the main team has stayed remarkably stable over the years, people of course move on: we remember with thanks and affection Jane Jeffes, our original Executive Producer/Editor, who, with Unique's Director of Programmes, Tim Blackmore, created *Something Understood*. Our first PA, and later Production Manager, Lucy Yeomans, brought a huge amount to the programme over a number of years, before being lured away to Manchester. Mark thanks his original producer, David Benedictus, for all he brought to the programme in its early days.

We thank Alison Mann, formerly of Unique, for all her hard work in ensuring this book happened, and Judith Longman, Editorial Director at Hodder & Stoughton, for taking the project on and for her encouragement and enthusiasm.

It's hard to know where we should have started this page, for *Something Understood* would never have been the success it has been without the support of a series of Controllers of BBC Radio 4, so we thank Michael Green, James Boyle and Helen Boaden, who have always given us the greatest encouragement. Tim Blackmore has met and negotiated with each controller in turn, and we thank him for his confidence in the programme, and for his continued quiet backing and guiding hand.

We would like to thank everyone at Unique for their continued support and commitment to the making of *Something Understood* and the producing of this book.

Finally, and perhaps most importantly of all, we thank our listeners, each and every one of them, for without them, there would be no *Something Understood*.

Mark Tully and Beverley McAinsh

→ 1 ←

They that love beyond the world

Yea, to such rashness, ratheness, rareness, ripeness, richness,
Love lures life on

They that love beyond the world

'*They that love beyond the world, cannot be separated by it. Death cannot kill what never dies.*' *These are the opening lines of one of our most requested readings ever, from the programme called '*Devotion*'. Written by William Penn, the seventeenth-century Quaker and founder of Pennsylvania, the poem gives voice to his conviction that true love and friendship transcend the grave.*

Love and friendship are constant themes in Something Understood, *touching as they do the deepest chords in the human heart. The readings which follow capture many of the shifting, shimmering facets of love, and of the special quality of friendship: the ebb and flow of passion; the quiet intimacy and soaring delight; the risks of disclosure and the fear of loss; the security, the humour, the healing; the jangling disturbance and exquisite peace. Some poets simply describe while others explore and analyse, but whatever their approach, their gift, to reader and listener alike, is to convey experience and insight which are both utterly unique and yet hauntingly recognisable. In capturing the reality of their own loves and friendships, they capture the shared hallmark of humanity.*

Darcy O'Farrell,
one of Mark Tully's oldest friends, speaking in 'Friendship'

Of course, the key to keeping in touch is that overused word 'communication'. You must keep in contact with people and you must make some sort of an effort. It's no use sitting around and waiting for the other fellow to come to you. And there's sometimes an element of sacrifice; you've got to be prepared to put things aside for your friend, some things that perhaps, superficially, you'd rather be doing. If someone you're really close to wants to see you, you have to be prepared to sacrifice your own plans to be with them.

I think because there is so much change and newness in life now, compared to when we were young, it's much easier to have superficial friendships with people and then forget about them when you pass onto the next new set. So I think it has become harder to retain and develop friendships because of the pace of life, but having said that, *real* friendship is a great rarity in life, and always has been.

The Little Language

When I am near you, I'm like a child,
I am still and simple, I am undefiled.
I speak my love in a forgotten tongue,
And use the words I knew when I was young.
My Love! You have restored me in a hundred ways,
You gave me back my happy childish days.

ANNA WICKHAM

Lines to a Movement in
Mozart's E-Flat Symphony

Show me again the time
When in the Junetide's prime
We flew by meads and mountains northerly! –
Yea, to such freshness, fairness, fulness, fineness, freeness,
Love lures life on.

Show me the day
When from the sandy bay
We looked together upon the pestered sea! –
Yea, to such surging, swaying, sighing, swelling, shrinking,
Love lures life on.

Show me again the hour
When by the pinnacled tower
We eyed each other and feared futurity! –
Yea, to such bodings, broodings, beatings, blanchings, blessings,
Love lures life on.

Show me again just this:
The moment of that kiss
Away from the prancing folk, by the strawberry-tree! –
Yea, to such rashness, ratheness, rareness, ripeness, richness,
Love lures life on.

THOMAS HARDY

Colours

When your face
appeared over my crumpled life
at first I understood
only the poverty of what I have.
Then its particular light
on woods, on rivers, on the sea,
became my beginning in the coloured world
in which I had not yet had my beginning.
I am so frightened, I am so frightened,
of the unexpected sunrise finishing,
of revelations
and tears and the excitement finishing.
I don't fight it, my love is this fear,
I nourish it who can nourish nothing,
love's slipshod watchman.
Fear hems me in.
I am conscious that these minutes are short
and that the colours in my eyes will vanish
when your face sets.

YEVGENY YEVTUSHENKO

The Shirt of a Lad

As I did the washing one day
Under the bridge at Aberteifi,
And a golden stick to drub it,
And my sweetheart's shirt beneath it –
A knight came by upon a charger,
Proud and swift and broad of shoulder,
And he asked if I would sell
The shirt of the lad that I loved well.

No, I said, I will not trade –
Not if a hundred pounds were paid;
Not if two hillsides I could keep
Full with wethers and white sheep;
Not if two fields full of oxen
Under yoke were in the bargain;
Not if the herbs of all Llanddewi,
Trodden and pressed, were offered to me –
Not for the likes of that, I'd sell
The shirt of the lad that I love well.

ANONYMOUS
translated by Tony Conran

Song of a Young Lady
to Her Ancient Lover

Ancient Person, for whom I,
All the flattering Youth defy;
Long be it e're thou grow Old,
Aking, shaking, Crazy Cold.
But still continue as thou art,
Ancient Person of my Heart.

On thy withered Lips and Dry,
Which like barren Furrows lye;
Brooding kisses I will pour
Shall thy youthful Heat restore.
Such kind Show'rs in Autumn fall,
And a second Spring recall:
Nor from thee will ever part,
Ancient Person of my Heart.

Thy Nobler parts which but to name
In our Sex wou'd be counted shame,
By Age's frozen grasp possest,
From their Ice shall be releast:
And, sooth'd by my reviving hand,
In former Warmth and Vigor stand.
All a Lover's wish can reach,
For thy Joy my Love shall teach:
And for thy Pleasure shall improve,
All that Art can add to Love.
Yet still I love thee without Art,
Ancient Person of my Heart.

JOHN WILMOT
THE EARL OF ROCHESTER

I Worry

I worry about you –
So long since we spoke.
Love, are you downhearted,
Dispirited, broke?

I worry about you.
I can't sleep at night.
Are you sad? Are you lonely?
Or are you alright?

They say that men suffer,
As badly, as long.
I worry, I worry,
In case they are wrong.

WENDY COPE

A Quoi Bon Dire

Seventeen years ago you said
   Something that sounded like Goodbye;
   And everybody thinks that you are dead,
      But I.

So I, as I grow stiff and cold
   To this and that say Goodbye too;
   And everybody sees that I am old
      But you.

   And one fine morning in a sunny lane
Some boy and girl will meet and kiss and swear
   That nobody can love their way again
      While over there
You will have smiled, I shall have tossed your hair.

CHARLOTTE MEW

XXX

Shake hands, we shall never be friends, all's over;
      I only vex you the more I try.
All's wrong that ever I've done or said,
And nought to help it in this dull head:
      Shake hands, here's luck, good-bye.

But if you come to a road where danger
      Or guilt or anguish or shame's to share,
Be good to the lad that loves you true
And the soul that was born to die for you,
      And whistle and I'll be there.

A. E. HOUSMAN

Friendship

Such love I cannot analyse;
It does not rest in lips or eyes,
Neither in kisses nor caress.
Partly, I know, it's gentleness

And understanding in one word
Or in brief letters. It's preserved
By trust and by respect and awe.
These are the words I'm feeling for.

Two people, yes, two lasting friends.
The giving comes, the taking ends.
There is no measure for such things.
For this all Nature slows and sings.

ELIZABETH JENNINGS

Identity

When I decide I shall assemble you
Or, more precisely, when I decide which thoughts
Of mine about you fit most easily together,
Then I can learn what I have loved, what lets
Light through the mind. The residue
Of what you may be goes. I gather

Only as lovers or friends gather at all
For making friends means this –
Image and passion combined into a whole
Pattern within the loving mind, not her or his
Concurring there. You can project the full
Picture of lover or friend that is not either.

So then assemble me,
Your exact picture firm and credible,
Though as I think myself I may be free
And accurate enough.
That you love what is truthful to your will
Is all that ever can be answered for
And, what is more,
Is all we make each other when we love.

ELIZABETH JENNINGS

They That Love Beyond the World

They that love beyond the world, cannot be separated by it.
Death cannot kill what never dies.
Nor can spirits ever be divided that love and live in the
same divine
   principle, the root and record of their friendship.
If absence be not death, neither is theirs.
Death is but crossing the world as friends do the seas;
they live in one
   another still.
For they must needs be present that love and live in that
which is omnipresent.
This is the comfort of friends, that though they may be said
to die, yet
   their friendship and society are ever present because
immortal.

WILLIAM PENN

Miraculous alchemy

UNDERSTANDING THE NATURAL WORLD

Glory be to God for dappled things —
  For skies of couple-colour as a brinded cow;
    For rose-moles all in stipple upon trout that swim;

Miraculous alchemy

The heart-stopping beauty of the natural world, and the sacredness which many recognise within its every atom, have been the evergreen themes of countless Something Understood*s: the turning seasons of the year; the fecund earth; the might of wind and wave; the grandeur of mountain and forest; the mystery of spinning planet and flickering star.*

These are favourite themes too in the work of some of our best-loved poets: William Wordsworth, Thomas Hardy, Laurie Lee, Gerard Manley Hopkins. These writers, and the others whose work is included here, bring to the natural world not only a penetrating gaze but a language and syntax so arresting that, through them, we see and sense our familiar world in new ways. In discovering new dimensions to the earth's beauty, we are reminded of our connection to it, our place in it, and our responsibility for it.

There is beauty and celebration in this chapter, but there is poignancy and warning too. Our loss of connection to the earth, and the damage and betrayal we inflict upon it, threaten the inheritance of generations.

The artist Luke Elwes,
speaking in 'Colour'

Colour is essential to me; it's the language I work with every day, rather as words are for the poet, or musical phrases for the musician. It's a way of trying to carry me back to the natural world and I think one of the interesting things about colour is that it's the way we can look at light in the natural world. Gerard Manley Hopkins writes in one of his poems about 'dappled' beauty and that dappling is the carrying of light through colour, and this, I think, is what colour is for above all, particularly for the artist but also for all of us. Colour is a way of seeing light in the world and understanding it. Light itself is colourless – you can't paint light, you can't paint dark – but you can use colour to point to both ends of the spectrum.

For me, all art has something of the sacred in it. I don't think it forms a definition of art: after all, a lot of conceptual art which we see today is a denial of the spiritual. It's an ironic, cool, detached statement about the world around us. It's not attempting to use the language of colour or line to take us beyond the natural appearance of things. But I feel, certainly, as a painter using colour, that it has the ability to carry, to transport the artist and the viewer beyond mere appearance. It's a fragile and difficult thing to do but it's something I think we all feel a need to do in our lives.

One of the glories of using colour is that you are trying to generate light – what Matisse called 'generating the luminous', and I think that in doing that you are talking about light as an equation with life, and as an equation with some sense of perfection or otherness which we all wish to touch in some form in our lives.

Hoar Frost

Miraculous alchemy! The hills appear
As if they'd suddenly been greyed by shock,
  Or drenched by spume of stars
  In some celestial storm.

Rimed is the spray to which the robin clings,
That loyal, valiant Knight of the burning shield,
  Who, riding astride a song,
  Gives battle to despair!

Hoar-tinselled poplars stand like morning ghosts,
And spikes of ice frill now the ivy leaf,
  And silver lamps festoon
  The swaying spider's web.

Caught in the larger net spun by the stars
All things are now – stone, grass, wild scrub and tree –
  Snared by a gemmed surprise
  Whose chill no pity knows.

Which stems the flowing sap, corrodes and kills
All unsuspecting fragile tenderness,
  But toughens what survives
  For fuller, stouter growth!

HUW MENAI

April Rise

If ever I saw blessing in the air
    I see it now in this still early day
Where lemon-green the vaporous morning drips
    Wet sunlight on the powder of my eye.

Blown bubble film of blue, the sky wraps round
    Weeds of warm light whose every root and rod
Splutters with soapy green, and all the world
    Sweats with the bead of summer in its bud.

If ever I heard blessing it is there
    Where birds in trees that shoals and shadows are
Splash with their hidden wings, and drops of sound
    Break on my ears their crests of throbbing air.

Pure in the haze the emerald sun dilates,
    The lips of mosses milk the spongy stones,
While white as water by the lake a girl
    Swims her green hand among the gathered swans.

Now, as the almond burns its smoking wick,
    Dropping small flames to light the candled grass;
Now, as my low blood scales its second chance,
    If ever world were blessed, now it is.

LAURIE LEE

Pied Beauty

Glory be to God for dappled things –
  For skies of couple-colour as a brinded cow;
    For rose-moles all in stipple upon trout that swim;
Fresh-firecoal chestnut-falls; finches wings;
  Landscape plotted and pieced – fold, fallow, and plough;
    And all trades, their gear and tackle and trim.

All things counter, original, spare, strange;
  Whatever is fickle, freckled (who knows how?)
    With swift, slow; sweet, sour; adazzle, dim;
He fathers-forth whose beauty is past change:
        Praise him.

GERARD MANLEY HOPKINS

God's Grandeur

The world is charged with the grandeur of God.
   It will flame out, like shining from shook foil;
   It gathers to a greatness, like the ooze of oil
Crushed. Why do men, then, now not reck his rod?
Generations have trod, have trod, have trod;
   And all is seared with trade; bleared, smeared with toil;
   And wears man's smudge and shares man's smell: the soil
Is bare now, nor can foot feel, being shod.

And for all this, nature is never spent;
   There lives the dearest freshness deep down things;
And though the last lights off the black west went
   Oh, morning, at the brown brink eastward, springs –
Because the Holy Ghost over the bent
   World broods with warm breast and with ah! bright wings.

GERARD MANLEY HOPKINS

Summer Moods

I love at eventide to walk alone
Down narrow lanes oerhung with dewy thorn
Where from the long grass underneath the snail
Jet black creeps out and sprouts his timid horn
I love to muse oer meadows newly mown
Where withering grass perfumes the sultry air
Where bees search round with sad and weary drone
In vain for flowers that bloomed but newly there
While in the juicey corn the hidden quail
Cries 'wet my foot' and hid as thoughts unborn
The fairy like and seldom-seen land rail
Utters 'craik craik' like voices underground
Right glad to meet the evenings dewy veil
And see the light fade into glooms around

JOHN CLARE

Seventh Day

Passive I lie, looking up through leaves,
An eye only, one of the eyes of earth
That open at a myriad points at the living surface.
Eyes that earth opens see and delight
Because of the leaves, because of the unfolding of the leaves.
The folding, veining, imbrication, fluttering, resting,
The green and deepening manifold of the leaves.

Eyes of the earth know only delight
Untroubled by anything that I am, and I am nothing:
All that nature is, receive and recognize,
Pleased with the sky, the falling water and the flowers
With bird and fish and the striations of stone.
Every natural form, living and moving
Delights these eyes that are no longer mine
That open upon earth and sky pure vision.
Nature sees, sees itself, is both seer and seen.

This is the divine repose, that watches
The ever-changing light and shadow, rock and sky and ocean.

KATHLEEN RAINE

Kilvert's Diary

Tuesday, 14th March

The afternoon had been stormy but it cleared towards sunset. Gradually the heavy rain clouds rolled across the valley to the foot of the opposite mountains and began climbing up their sides wreathing in rolling masses of vapour. One solitary cloud still hung over the brilliant sunlit town, and that whole cloud was a rainbow. Gradually it lost its bright prismatic hues and moved away up the Cusop Dingle in the shape of a pillar and of the colour of golden dark smoke. The Black Mountains were invisible, being wrapped in clouds, and I saw one very white brilliant cloud where the mountains ought to have been. This cloud grew more white and dazzling every moment, till a clearer burst of sunlight scattered the mists and revealed the truth. This brilliant white cloud that I had been looking and wondering at was the mountain in snow. The last cloud and mist rolled away over the mountain tops and the mountains stood up in the clear blue heaven, a long rampart line of dazzling glittering snow so as no fuller on earth can white them. I stood rooted to the ground, struck with amazement and overwhelmed at the extraordinary splendour of this marvellous spectacle. I never saw anything to equal it I think, even among the high Alps. One's first involuntary thought in the presence of these magnificent sights is to lift up the heart to God and humbly thank Him for having made the earth so beautiful. An intense glare of primrose light streamed from the west deepening into rose and crimson. There was not a flake of snow anywhere but on the mountains and they stood up, the great white range rising high into the blue sky, while all the rest of the world at their feet lay ruddy rosy brown. The sudden contrast was tremendous, electrifying. I could have cried with the excitement of the overwhelming spectacle.

THE REVEREND FRANCIS KILVERT

We Who Were Born

We who were born
In country places,
Far from cities
And shifting faces,
We have a birthright
No man can sell,
And a secret joy
No man can tell.

For we are kindred
To lordly things,
The wild duck's flight
And the white owl's wings;
To pike and salmon,
To bull and horse,
The curlew's cry
And the smell of gorse.

Pride of trees,
Swiftness of streams,
Magic of frost
Have shaped our dreams:
No baser vision
Their spirit fills
Who walk by right
On the naked hills.

EILUNED LEWIS

Chief Seathl's Testament

Every part of this earth is sacred to my people.
Every shining pine needle, every sandy shore, every mist
in the dark wood, every clearing and humming
insect is holy in the memory and experience of my people.
The sap which courses through the trees
carries the memories of the red man.

The white man's dead forget the country of their birth
when they go to walk among the stars.
Our dead never forget this beautiful earth,
For it is the mother of the red man.
We are part of the earth and it is part of us.
The perfumed flowers are our sisters; the deer,
the horse, the great eagle, these are our brothers.
The rocky crests, the juices in the meadow, the body heat
of the pony and man – all belong to the same family.
So when the Great Chief in Washington sends word
that he wishes to buy our land, he asks much of us.
The Great Chief sends word he will reserve us a place
so that we can live comfortably to ourselves.
He will be our father and we will be his children.
So we will consider your offer to buy our land.
But it will not be easy for this land is sacred to us.
This shining water that moves in
streams and the rivers is not just
water but the blood of our ancestors.

CHIEF SEATHL

Trees

Consider the life of trees.

Aside from the axe, what trees acquire from man is inconsiderable.

What man may acquire from trees is immeasurable.

From their mute forms there flows a poise in silence;

a lovely sound and motion in response to wind.

What peace comes to those aware of the voice and bearing

of trees!

Trees do not scream for attention.

A tree, a rock, has no pretence, only a real growth out of itself,

in close communion with the universal spirit.

A tree retains a deep serenity.

It establishes in the earth not only its root system but also

those roots of its beauty and its unknown consciousness.

Sometimes one may sense a glisten of that consciousness,

and with

such perspective, feel that man is not necessarily the highest

form of life.

CEDRIC WRIGHT

The Music of the Spheres

The bodies of gaseous spheres that we call *stars*
kept together and lit by their own gravity.
     Their light is nakedness says Rubén,
      who brought harmony from the sacred wood.
Suppose, reader, we want to see star HK193182.
     The star could not see its beauty
     unless we did.
We are the star seeing itself.
Born in its fire
and cooled to be able to think and see.
Protons, neutrons and electrons
are the human body, the planet and the stars.
From the unconscious consciousness came
so in us the planet loves and dreams.
It is the Earth singing this *Cosmic Canticle* in me.

        The music of the spheres.

'The spheres are not the planets
     but electrons and atomic nuclei
and the music is not sound but light.'
         $E = mc^2$
Photons – light particles –
The ether's violins throbbed its clarity
according to Alfonso.
'If our eyes were more perfect
we would see the atoms singing.'
     They say the proton sounds like a Bach fugue.

ERNESTO CARDENAL

September 1815

While not a leaf seems faded, – while the fields,
With ripening harvests prodigally fair,
In brightest sunshine bask, – this nipping air,
Sent from some distant clime where Winter wields
His icy scymetar, a foretaste yields
Of bitter change – and bids the Flowers beware;
And whispers to the silent Birds, 'prepare
Against the threatening Foe your trustiest shields.'
For me, who under kindlier laws belong
To Nature's tuneful quire this rustling dry
Through the green leaves, and yon crystalline sky,
Announce a season potent to renew,
Mid frost and snow, the instinctive joys of song,
And nobler cares than listless summer knew.

WILLIAM WORDSWORTH

The Darkling Thrush

I leant upon a coppice gate
    When Frost was spectre-grey,
And Winter's dregs made desolate
    The weakening eye of day.
The tangled bine-stems scored the sky
    Like strings of broken lyres,
And all mankind that haunted nigh
    Had sought their household fires.

The land's sharp features seem'd to be
    The Century's corpse outleant,
His crypt the cloudy canopy,
    The wind his death-lament.
The ancient pulse of germ and birth
    Was shrunken hard and dry,
And every spirit upon earth
    Seem'd fervourless as I.

At once a voice arose among
    The bleak twigs overhead
In a full-hearted evensong
    Of joy illimited;
An agèd thrush, frail, gaunt, and small,
    In blast-beruffled plume,
Had chosen thus to fling his soul
    Upon the growing gloom.

So little cause for carollings
    Of such ecstatic sound
Was written on terrestrial things
    Afar or nigh around,
That I could think there trembled through
    His happy good-night air
Some blessèd Hope, whereof he knew
    And I was unaware.

THOMAS HARDY

→ *3* ←

And I to my pledged word am true

> *To be great, be entire: of what's yours nothing*
> *Exaggerate or exclude.*
> *Be whole in each thing. Put all that you are*
> *Into the least you do.*

And I to my pledged word am true

Courage, integrity, creativity, strength and vision: these, the very best of human qualities, run like seams of light through Something Understood. *The details of time and place, people and circumstance, may vary endlessly, but the qualities remain constant, closely woven but distinct, inspiring us in turn to be the best that we can be.*

In 'The Truly Great', Stephen Spender writes of those

> Who, from the womb, remembered the soul's history
> Through corridors of light …
> Born of the sun, they travelled a short while toward the sun
> And left the vivid air signed with their honour.

Many of those who have written or inspired the pieces in this chapter have signed the air with their honour*: the war poets Alan Seeger and Siegfried Sassoon, the Chilean writer Maria Eugenia Bravo Calderara, and the Burmese opposition leader Aung San Suu Kyi. The human spirit shines brightest in the resilience and hope of these men and women, and in their prophetic courage within and beyond their suffering.*

But courage, integrity and strength are also essential in the quieter, private quest to be true to one's self and one's calling. D. H. Lawrence struggles to be the best he can be *in the 'Song of a Man Who has Come Through', and Fernando Pessoa's 'To Be Great, Be Entire' offers simple but rigorous advice to us all. Our calling may not be that of the scientist, or the poet, the nun or the mystic, but whatever it is and wherever it leads us, his exhortation is the same: 'To be great, be entire … Put all that you are into the least you do.'*

37

Philip Sheldrake, Vice Principal of Sarum College and writer on spirituality, speaking in 'Desire'

I actually believe that 'desire' is the doorway into our deepest identity. If we look at our desires we will learn a great deal about the kind of people we most truly are. Therefore if we attend to our desires, over time, and with judgment and discernment, I think we'll discover the directions our lives should take, and that from within rather than something imposed from outside.

Desire for me also stands for something pushing us to exceed the place where we are, and in that sense it's a very active word: it's about movement, about process, and about growth.

I know that, at the very least, people experience a conflict of desires. But the only way we can really learn the truth of our desires is by attending to them, not by trying to work out in the abstract where they come from but perhaps by asking ourselves where would they lead if we were to follow them through. Then you begin to see that certain desires, if we really lived our lives according to them, would lead us to become more fragmented as people, more selfish, more angry, less peaceful ... and other desires, if we followed them through, clearly would lead much more towards harmony, unity, peace ... in that very simple way you can begin to see which desires are most life-giving and central.

I do think that one of the parts of the human journey is to realise that self-fulfilment is never self-centredness. Those two things are often confused, but self-centredness – that which essentially separates me off from the interests of other people, putting me first, middle and last in an almost exclusive way – is not, in truth, self-fulfilment. All true desire, I believe, does in the end enable us to transcend ourselves in the sense of the selfish self, the limited self. It is an invitation always to move out of self, in an act of vulnerability.

The Truly Great

I think continually of those who were truly great.
Who, from the womb, remembered the soul's history
Through corridors of light, where the hours are suns,
Endless and singing. Whose lovely ambition
Was that their lips, still touched with fire,
Should tell of the Spirit, clothed from head to foot in song.
And who hoarded from the Spring branches
The desires falling across their bodies like blossoms.

What is precious, is never to forget.
The essential delight of the blood drawn from ageless springs
Breaking through rocks in worlds before our earth.
Never to deny its pleasure in the morning simple light
Nor its grave evening demand for love.
Never to allow gradually the traffic to smother
With noise and fog, the flowering of the spirit.

Near the snow, near the sun, in the highest fields,
See how these names are fêted by the waving grass
And by the streamers of white cloud
And whispers of wind in the listening sky.
The names of those who in their lives fought for life,
Who wore at their hearts the fire's centre.
Born of the sun, they travelled a short while toward the sun
And left the vivid air signed with their honour.

STEPHEN SPENDER

I Have a Rendezvous with Death …

I have a rendezvous with Death
At some disputed barricade,
When Spring comes back with rustling shade
And apple-blossoms fill the air –
I have a rendezvous with Death
When Spring brings back blue days and fair.

It may be he shall take my hand
And lead me into his dark land
And close my eyes and quench my breath –
It may be I shall pass him still.
I have a rendezvous with Death
On some scarred slope of battered hill,
When Spring comes round again this year
And the first meadow-flowers appear.

God knows 'twere better to be deep
Pillowed in silk and scented down,
Where love throbs out in blissful sleep,
Pulse nigh to pulse, and breath to breath,
Where hushed awakenings are dear …
But I've a rendezvous with Death
At midnight in some flaming town,
When Spring trips north again this year,
And I to pledged word am true,
I shall not fail that rendezvous.

ALAN SEEGER

The Power and the Glory

Let there be life, said God. And what He wrought
Went past in myriad marching lives, and brought
This hour, this quiet room, and my small thought
Holding invisible vastness in its hands.

Let there be God, say I. And what I've done
Goes onward like the splendour of the sun
And rises up in rapture and is one
With the white power of conscience that commands.

Let life be God ...What wail of fiend or wraith
Dare mock my glorious angel where he stands
To fill my dark with fire, my heart with faith?

SIEGFRIED SASSOON

In Memory of Anne Frank

Röslein auf dem Heiden

Larch, gorse, rough grass,
heather, bracken, moss,
wild rose on the heath –
bare from bony feet,
fouled, burned – recreate
beauty, breed out of death,
carpet again the heath
where once, between rose
and larch, Hell was.

Life is sweet,
as you did not forget
living, never let
fear or horror deny it;
so now, dead, can teach
our doubt and shame – sweet
day and night,
cloud and sun, stars,
wind on the heath.

MARTIN ROBERTSON

The People of Orpheus

You may not know this: the ones
who have gone like Orpheus
down to the regions of hell,
have a bond between them, much
stronger than blood.

These people, holding in
past agonies, have learned
to build their own happiness
little by little.

You'll know them: a certain kind
of tiredness around
eyes that are smiling;
the way they laugh, the whole
of life in their laughter, all
its terrifying brightness
on the border with death.

No one can laugh like them.
They know they've lived on.
And now listen to me well
hear what I say:
they are the only people
who know the path to Paradise.

MARÍA EUGENIA BRAVO CALDERARA
translated by Ruth Valentine and Erif Reson

Freedom from Fear

The effort necessary to remain uncorrupted in an environment where fear is an integral part of everyday existence is not immediately apparent to those fortunate enough to live in states governed by the rule of law. Just laws do not merely prevent corruption by meting out impartial punishment to offenders. They also help to create a society in which people can fulfil the basic requirements necessary for the preservation of human dignity without recourse to corrupt practices. Where there are no such laws, the burden of upholding the principles of justice and common decency falls on the ordinary people. It is the cumulative effect of their sustained effort and steady endurance which will change a nation where reason and conscience are warped by fear into one where legal rules exist to promote man's desire for harmony and justice while restraining the less desirable destructive traits in his nature …

… Saints, it has been said, are the sinners who go on trying. So free men are the oppressed who go on trying and who in the process make themselves fit to bear the responsibilities and to uphold the disciplines which will maintain a free society. Among the basic freedoms to which men aspire that their lives might be full and uncramped, freedom from fear stands out as both a means and an end. A people who would build a nation in which strong, democratic institutions are firmly established as a guarantee against state-induced power must first learn to liberate their own minds from apathy and fear.

AUNG SAN SUU KYI

The Poet

He is a link between this and the coming world. He is
A pure spring from which all thirsty souls may drink.

He is a tree watered by the River of Beauty, bearing
Fruit which the hungry heart craves;
He is a nightingale, soothing the depressed
Spirit with his beautiful melodies;
He is a white cloud appearing over the horizon,
Ascending and growing until it fills the face of the sky.
Then it falls on the flowers in the Field of Life,
Opening their petals to admit the light.

He is an angel, sent by the goddess to
Preach the Deity's gospel;
He is a brilliant lamp, unconquered by darkness
And inextinguishable by the wind. It is filled with
Oil by Ishtar of Love, and lighted by Apollon of Music.

He is a solitary figure, robed in simplicity and
Kindness; He sits upon the lap of Nature to draw his
Inspiration, and stays up in the silence of the night,
Awaiting the descending of the spirit.

He is a sower who sows the seeds of his heart in the
Prairies of affection, and humanity reaps the
Harvest for her nourishment.

This is the poet – whom the people ignore in this life,
And who is recognised only after he bids the earthly
World farewell and returns to his arbour in heaven.

This is the poet – who asks naught of
Humanity but a smile.
This is the poet – whose spirit ascends and
Fills the firmament with beautiful sayings;
Yet the people deny themselves his radiance.

Until when shall the people remain asleep?
Until when shall they continue to glorify those
Who attained greatness by moments of advantage?
How long shall they ignore those who enable
Them to see the beauty of their spirit,
Symbol of peace and love?
Until when shall human beings honour the dead
And forget the living, who spend their lives
Encircled in misery, and who consume themselves
Like burning candles to illuminate the way
For the ignorant and lead them into the path of light?

Poet, you are the life of this life, and you have
Triumphed over the ages despite their severity.

Poet, you will one day rule the hearts, and
Therefore, your kingdom has no ending.
Poet, examine your crown of thorns; you will
Find concealed in it a budding wreath of laurel.

KAHLIL GIBRAN

Success in Malaria Research

This day relenting God
   Hath placed within my hand
A wondrous thing; and God
   Be praised. At his command,

Seeking His secret deeds
   With tears and toiling breath,
I find thy cunning seeds,
   O million-murdering Death.

I know this little thing
   A myriad men will save.
O Death, where is thy sting?
   Thy victory, O Grave?

SIR RONALD ROSS

To Be Great, Be Entire

To be great, be entire: of what's yours nothing
    Exaggerate or exclude.
Be whole in each thing. Put all that you are
    Into the least you do.
Like that on each place the whole moon
    Shines, for she lives aloft.

FERNANDO PESSOA
translated by Jonathan Griffin

The Heart of a Child

Grant me, O God,
    the heart of a child,
pure and transparent as a spring;
    a simple heart,
which never harbours sorrows;
a heart glorious in self-giving,
    tender in compassion;
a heart faithful and generous,
which will never forget any good
or bear a grudge for any evil.

Make me a heart gentle and humble,
    loving without asking any return,
    largehearted and undauntable,
which no ingratitude can sour
and no indifference can weary;
    a heart penetrated by the love of Jesus
    whose desire will only be
       satisfied in heaven.

Grant me, O Lord,
    the mind and heart
    of thy dear Son.

GEORGE APPLETON

Conversion

He was a born loser,
accident-prone too;
never won a lottery,
married a girl who
couldn't cook, broke
his leg the day before
the wedding
and forgot the ring.
He was the kind
who ended up behind a post
in almost any
auditorium. Planes
he was booked to fly on
were delayed
by engine trouble
with sickening regularity.
His holidays at the beach
were almost always
ruined by rain. All
his apples turned out
wormy. His letters
came back marked
'Moved, left no
address.' And it was
his car that was cited
for speeding
from among a flock of others
going 60 in a
55 mile zone.

So it was a real shocker
when he found himself
elected, chosen by Grace
for Salvation, felt
the exhilaration of
an undeserved and wholly
unexpected joy
and tasted, for the
first time, the Glory
of being on
the winning side.

LUCI SHAW

A Nun on the Platform

She seems in place here,
as much as in the convent,
self-contained, neat.
You could hardly call it luggage.

No frantic balancing of cups,
but like a swan, which also
has no hands for magazines,
she stands complete.

No intermediate, half unsureness,
no drawing kids back from the edge,
or disappointment over missing,
or expectation of arrival

of a train, lean her,
like the rest of us, out of true.
We are all some distance from our roots
on this platform, but she seems at home,

as her Sisters will be
in the over large garden
reaching for tall fruits,
their thoughts ripening for pardon.

Seeing a nun on a platform
gives the day a jolt,
like an act of kindness,
or a pain that halts.

DAVID SCOTT

Song of a Man Who Has Come Through

Not I, not I, but the wind that blows through me!
A fine wind is blowing the new direction of Time.
If only I let it bear me, carry me, if only it carry me!
If only I am sensitive, subtle, oh, delicate, a winged gift!
If only, most lovely of all, I yield myself and am borrowed
By the fine, fine wind that takes its course through the
    chaos of the world
Like a fine, an exquisite chisel, a wedge-blade inserted;
If only I am keen and hard like the sheer tip of a wedge
Driven by invisible blows,
The rock will split, we shall come at the wonder, we shall
    find the Hesperides.

Oh, for the wonder that bubbles into my soul,
I would be a good fountain, a good well-head,
Would blur no whisper, spoil no expression.

What is the knocking?
What is the knocking at the door in the night?
It is somebody wants to do us harm.

No, no, it is the three strange angels.
Admit them, admit them.

D. H. LAWRENCE

When My Lord Comes …

When my Lord comes
I am beside myself
For there cometh with Him such sweet melody
That all carnal desire dieth within me:
And His sweet music puts far from me
All sorrow of heart.
The mighty voice of the Godhead
Has spoken to me in powerful words
Which I have received
With the dull hearing of my misery –
A light of utmost splendour
Glows on the eyes of my soul
Therein have I seen the inexpressible ordering
Of all things, and recognised God's unspeakable glory –
That incomprehensible wonder –
The tender caress between God and the soul,
The sufficiency in the Highest,
Discipline in understanding,
Realisation with withdrawal,
According to the power of the senses,
The unmingled joy of union.
The living love of Eternity
As it now is and evermore shall be.

MECHTILD OF MAGDEBURG

→→ **4** ←←

Is this where God hides?

UNDERSTANDING THE QUEST FOR GOD

... nought shall conquer or control
The heavenward hunger of our soul

Is this where God hides?

In our programme called 'Surprise, Surprise', Father Gerard Hughes said: 'God is a beckoning word'. The poems and stories in this chapter are drawn from many faiths and traditions, ages and cultures: Buddhist, Sufi, Hasidic; Catholic, Protestant; rational; mystical. Each tradition expresses its ideas about God or the Ultimate in strikingly different images and analogies. Yet more striking, even than that colourful diversity, is an underlying similarity: the sense of recognition and familiarity that stirs the spirit as writer after writer explores what it means to respond to the beckoning finger of God.

The deep yearning and conviction that fuel the quest for God; the difficulties and doubts along the way; the discipline and determination to be mustered; the confusing and inexplicable withdrawal of the divine presence; the tantalising glimpses and moments of joyous consummation; the learning to be at peace with 'the now and the not yet', with knowing only in part, with seeing only through dark glass. All these are familiar experiences to those embarked upon the quest for God; those who, like the writers here, are driven ever onwards by the hunger of their soul.

Mary Pat Fisher, writer, and member of the Gobind Sadan community in Delhi, speaking in 'People of the Book'

A mystic looks for truth in a different kind of way than a person who believes in a religion in an outward way. A mystic is always digging, digging: trying to face the self and find that which transcends all our worldly concepts. The absolute truth is something which one approaches only by disappearing and becoming as nothing. Kabir says that God is like sugar scattered in the sand: an elephant cannot grasp it; become like an ant and partake of it.

Father Gerard Hughes,
speaking in 'Surprise, Surprise'

God is most easily, if painfully, found when we lose our securities. And when the really profound securities go you're left either with despair or with the question: 'Is there anything?', and I think it's there, that glimpse of God, when everything else seems to have gone.

God, of God's very nature, is beyond our thinking or imagining. God goes before his people, a pillar of cloud; God is always ahead of us. I love that description: 'God is a beckoning word', calling us out from ourselves. God is the transcendent one; God cannot be domesticated, can't be tamed, can't be enclosed or defined. And that's the exciting thing in God; that's why the Church calls itself the Pilgrim People: it's on a journey, it hasn't arrived yet, it's still wandering. But the heart knows which direction to go.

Searching for God

Lord, where shall I find You?
High and hidden is Your place.
And where shall I not find You?
The World is full of Your glory.

I have sought Your nearness,
with all my heart I called You
and going out to meet You
I found You coming to meet me.

JUDAH HALEVI

Only God I Saw

In the market, in the cloister – only God I saw.
In the valley and on the mountain – only God I saw.
Him I have seen beside me oft in tribulation;
In favour and in fortune – only God I saw.
In prayer and fasting, in praise and contemplation,
In the religion of the Prophet – only God I saw.
I oped mine eyes and by the light of his face around me
In all the eye discovered – only God I saw.
Like a candle I was melting in his fire:
Amidst the flames outlashing – only God I saw.
Myself with mine own eyes I saw most clearly,
But when I looked with God's eyes – only God I saw.
I passed away into nothingness, I vanished,
And lo, I was the All-living – only God I saw.

'BÁBÁ KÚHÍ OF SHÍRÁZ'
translated by R. A. Nicholson

The Seekers

Friends and loves we have none, nor wealth nor blessed abode,
But the hope of the City of God at the other end of the road.

Not for us are content, and quiet, and peace of mind,
For we go seeking a city that we shall never find.

There is no solace on earth for us – for such as we –
Who search for a hidden city that we shall never see.

Only the road and the dawn, the sun, the wind, and the rain,
And the watch-fire under the stars, and sleep, and the road again.

We seek the City of God, and the haunt where beauty dwells,
And we find the noisy mart and the sound of burial bells.

Never the golden city, where radiant people meet,
But the dolorous town where mourners are going about the street.

We travel the dusty road till the light of the day is dim,
And sunset shows us spires away on the world's rim.

We travel from dawn to dusk till the day is past and by,
Seeking the Holy City beyond the rim of the sky.

Friends and loves we have none, nor wealth nor blest abode,
But the hope of the City of God at the other end of the road.

JOHN MASEFIELD

To a Buddha Seated on a Lotus

Lord Buddha, on thy Lotus-throne,
With praying eyes and hands elate,
What mystic rapture dost thou own,
Immutable and ultimate?
What peace, unravished of our ken,
Annihilate from the world of men?

The wind of change for ever blows
Across the tumult of our way,
To-morrow's unborn griefs depose
The sorrow of our yesterday.
Dream yields to dream, strife follows strife,
And Death unweaves the webs of Life.

For us the travail and the heat,
The broken secrets of our pride,
The strenuous lessons of defeat,
The flower deferred, the fruit denied;
But not the peace, supremely won,
Lord Buddha, of thy Lotus-throne.

With futile hands we seek to gain
Our inaccessible desire,
Diviner summits to attain,
With faith that sinks and feet that tire
But nought shall conquer or control
The heavenward hunger of our soul.

The end, elusive and afar,
Still lures us with its beckoning flight,
And all our mortal moments are
A session of the Infinite.
How shall we reach the great, unknown
Nirvana of thy Lotus-throne?

SAROJINI NAYADU

The Kingdom of God

In No Strange Land

O world invisible, we view thee,
O world intangible, we touch thee,
O world unknowable, we know thee,
Inapprehensible, we clutch thee!

Does the fish soar to find the ocean,
The eagle plunge to find the air —
That we ask of the stars in motion
If they have rumour of thee there?

Not where the wheeling systems darken,
And our benumbed conceiving soars! —
The drift of pinions, would we hearken,
Beats at our own clay-shuttered doors.

The angels keep their ancient places; —
Turn but a stone, and start a wing!
'Tis ye, 'tis your estrangèd faces,
That miss the many-splendoured thing.

But (when so sad thou canst not sadder)
Cry; — and upon thy so sore loss
Shall shine the traffic of Jacob's ladder
Pitched betwixt Heaven and Charing Cross.

Yea, in the night, my Soul, my daughter,
Cry, — clinging Heaven by the hems;
And lo, Christ walking on the water
Not of Gennesareth, but Thames!

FRANCIS THOMPSON

The Measure of Love

If love be strong, hot, mighty and fervènt,
There may no trouble, grief or sorrow fall,
But that the lover would be well content
All to endure and think it eke too small,
Though it were death, so he might therewithal
The joyful presence of that person get
On whom he hath his heart and love y-set.

Thus should of God the lover be content
Any distress or sorrow to endure,
Rather than to be from God absènt,
And glad to die, so that he may be sure,
By his departing hence for to procure,
After this valley dark, the heavenly light,
And of his love the glorious blessed sight.

Not only a lover content is in his heart
But coveteth eke and longeth to sustain
Some labour, incommodity, or smart,
Loss, adversity, trouble, grief or pain:
And of his sorrow, joyful is and fain.
And happy thinketh himself that he may take
Some misadventure for his lover's sake.

Thus shouldest thou, that lovest God also,
In thine heart wish, covet, and be glad
For him to suffer trouble, pain and woe:
For whom if thou be never so woe bestead,
Yet thou ne shalt sustain (be not adread)
Half the dolour, grief and adversity
That he already suffered hath for thee.

SIR THOMAS MORE

A Buddhist Poem

He who is Blessing passed by my hut,
passed me, the barber. *
I ran and he turned, waited
for me, the barber!
I said, 'May I speak to you, Lord?'
He said, 'Yes.'
'Yes,' to *me*, the barber!
I said, 'Can your Peace be for a person like me?'
He said, 'Yes.'
His Peace for *me*, the barber!
I said, 'May I follow you, Lord?'
He said, 'Yes,'
to *me*, the barber!
I said, 'May I stay close to you, Lord?'
He said, 'You may,'
close to *me*, the poor barber!

ANONYMOUS

* Traditionally in India a barber was an 'untouchable'.

A Hasidic Tale

Late one evening a poor farmer on his way back from the market found himself without his prayer book. The wheel of his cart had come off right in the middle of the woods and it distressed him that this day should pass without his having said his prayers.

So this is the prayer he made: 'I have done something very foolish, Lord. I came away from home this morning without my prayer book and my memory is such that I cannot recite a single prayer without it. So this is what I am going to do: I shall recite the alphabet five times very slowly and you, to whom all prayers are known, can put the letters together to form the prayers I can't remember.'

And the Lord said to his angels, 'Of all the prayers I have heard today, this one was undoubtedly the best because it came from a heart that was simple and sincere.'

RETOLD BY ANTHONY DE MELLO

Ordinary God

'Do you believe in a God
who can change the course of events
on earth?'
                    'No, just
the ordinary one.'
                              A laugh,
but not so stupid: events
He does not, it seems, determine
for the most part. Whether He could
is not to the point; it is not
stupid to believe in
a God who mostly abjures.

The ordinary kind
of God is what one believes in
so implicitly that
it is only with blushes or
bravado one can declare,
'I believe'; caught as one is
in the ambush of personal history, so
harried, so distraught.

The ordinary kind
Of undeceived believer
expects no prompt reward
from an ultimately faithful
but meanwhile preoccupied landlord.

DONALD DAVIE

In Church

Often I try
To analyse the quality
Of its silences. Is this where God hides
From my searching? I have stopped to listen,
After the few people have gone,
To the air recomposing itself
For vigil. It has waited like this
Since the stones grouped themselves about it.
These are the hard ribs
Of a body that our prayers have failed
To animate. Shadows advance
From their corners to take possession
Of places the light held
For an hour. The bats resume
Their business. The uneasiness of the pews
Ceases. There is no other sound
In the darkness but the sound of a man
Breathing, testing his faith
On emptiness, nailing his questions
One by one to an untenanted cross.

R. S. THOMAS

A Julian Contemplation

Be silent.
Be still.
Wait before your God.
Say nothing.
Ask nothing.
Be still.
Let your God look upon you.
That is all.
God knows.
God understands.
God loves you with an enormous love.
God only wants to look upon you with love.
Quiet.
Still.
Be.
Let your God love you.

EDWINA GATELEY

The Secret of the Universe

An Ode by a Western Spinning Dervish

I spin, I spin, around, around,
    And close my eyes,
    And let the bile arise
From the sacred region of the soul's Profound;
Then gaze upon the world; how strange! how new!
    The earth and heaven are one,
    The horizon-line is gone,
The sky how green! the land how fair and blue!
Perplexing items fade from my large view,
And thought which vexed me with its false and true
Is swallowed up in Intuition; this,
    This is the sole true mode
    Of reaching God,
And gaining the universal synthesis
Which makes All – One; while fools with peering eyes
Dissect, divide, and vainly analyse.
So round, and round, and round again!
How the whole globe swells within my brain,
The stars inside my lids appear,
The murmur of the spheres I hear
Throbbing and beating in each ear;
Right in my navel I can feel
The centre of the world's great wheel.
Ah peace divine, bliss dear and deep,
    No stay, no stop,
    Like any top
Whirling with swiftest speed, I sleep.

O ye devout ones round me coming,
Listen! I think that I am humming;
      No utterance of the servile mind
With poor chop-logic rules agreeing
      Here shall ye find,
But inarticulate burr of man's unsundered being.
Ah, could we but devise some plan,
Some patent jack by which a man
Might hold himself ever in harmony
With the great whole, and spin perpetually,
      As all things spin
      Without, within,
As Time spins off into Eternity,
And space into the inane Immensity,
And the Finite into God's Infinity,
      Spin, spin, spin, spin.

EDWARD DOWDEN

Lost and Found

I missed him when the sun began to bend;
I found him not when I had lost his rim;
With many tears I went in search of him,
Climbing high mountains which did still ascend,
And gave me echoes when I called my friend;
Through cities vast and charnel-houses grim,
And high cathedrals where the light was dim,
Through books and arts and works without an end,
But found him not – the friend whom I had lost.
And yet I found him – as I found the lark,
A sound in fields I heard but could not mark:
I found him nearest when I missed him most;
I found him in my heart, a life in frost,
A light I knew not till my soul was dark.

GEORGE MACDONALD

Upon the Crucifix

Now I have found thee I will evermore
Embrace this standard where thou sitts above,
Feede greedie eies, and from hence never rove;
Sucke hungrie soule of this eternall store;
And lett my lippes from kissinge not remove.
O that I weare transformed into love,
And as a plant might springe uppon this flower,
Like wandring Ivy or sweete honnie suckle:
How would I with my twine about it buckle,
And kisse his feete with my ambitious boughes,
And clyme along uppon his sacred brest,
And make a garland for his wounded browes:
Lord soe I am, if heare my thoughts may rest.

WILLIAM ALABASTER

➤➤ 5 ◄◄

I'll hold your hand

UNDERSTANDING YOUTH AND AGE

The greatest dreams on earth
I trust to you my child.
You are the seed of humankind,
the hope, the future of the world.

I'll hold your hand

Some of the most poignant readings in this collection appear here, as writers such as *Victor Hugo, Jeni Couzyn, Stephen Spender, Vernon Scannell* and *Trán Ðúc Uyén* articulate their enchantment with their children, their sense of responsibility and fierce protectiveness towards them and the hopes and dreams they cherish for them. There are haunting evocations of mortality as poets struggle with the swiftness of their child's passing from infant to child and from child to adult, or, more starkly still, with the scandal of a child's suffering and death, overturning the natural order and leaving a crushing legacy of grief and confusion.

But the words 'I'll hold your hand' come not from a parent's offer to a child, but that of a small child to an old woman, in a poem by *Margaret Cropper.* Vulnerable and afraid, she is rescued when, with unobtrusive thoughtfulness, the child provides a steadying hand. It is a touching image of that warm and unselfconscious affinity that can connect the very young and very old.

There is wisdom here too: the different wisdoms of youth and age; the wisdom passed on from generation to generation, some of it welcomed, some, sadly, despised; and the wisdom of *Kahlil Gibran,* in the words of The Prophet:

> And a woman who held a babe against her bosom said, Speak to
> us of Children.
>
> And he said:
>
> Your children are not your children.
>
> They are the sons and daughters of Life's longing for itself.

Sarah Settelen, speaking in 'Unconditional Love', about her daughter Ellie. Ellie suffered from multiple disabilities and died at the age of 4

There's no doubt at all that I loved Ellie; I loved her from the moment she was born. But the process she took me through to get to the point of being able to love her *unconditionally* was a process whereby she challenged my sense of self; she challenged my ego and all my illusions about the reality that I had built up around me. I realised that I was defining myself in relationship to other people, and their responses to me, and because I was defining myself so much in terms of other people, I couldn't love Ellie without conditions. I had so many needs, needs that, because of her condition, she wasn't able to fulfil. So what I had to learn from Ellie was that those needs had to be fulfilled within myself.

I don't think, now, that any of us are able to love anyone else unconditionally until we can love ourselves unconditionally, and that is the process Ellie took me through. She taught me to stop relating to myself and defining myself through other people; to love myself without any expectations and completely unconditionally, and then I was able to love her unconditionally. Unconditional love is incredibly liberating.

Dawn

Of your hand I could say this
a bird poised mid-air in flight
as delicate and smooth.

Of your mouth
a foxglove in its taking
without edges or hurt.

This of your ear
a sea-horse, immortal
sporting in white waves

and of your eye
a place where no one could hide
nothing lurk.

Of your cupped flesh
smooth on my palm
an agate on the sea-shore.

Of your back and belly
that they command kisses.
I would say of your feet

they're inquisitive and fleet
as squirrels or birds
and so return to your hand

beginning my voyage
around your loveliness
again and yet again

as in my arms you lie sleeping.

JENI COUZYN

To My Daughter

Bright clasp of her whole hand around my finger,
My daughter, as we walk together now.
All my life I'll feel a ring invisibly
Circle this bone with shining: when she is grown
Far from today as her eyes are already.

STEPHEN SPENDER

To His Son, Vincent Corbet, on His Third Birthday

What I shall leave thee none can tell,
But all shall say I wish thee well;
I wish thee, Vin, before all wealth,
Both bodily and ghostly health:
Nor too much wealth, nor wit, come to thee.
So much of either may undo thee.
I wish thee learning, not for show,
Enough for to instruct and know;
Not such as gentlemen require,
To prate at table or at fire.
I wish thee all thy mother's graces,
Thy father's fortunes, and his places.
I wish thee friends, and one at court,
Not to build on, but support;
To keep thee, not in doing many
Oppressions, but from suffering any.
I wish thee peace in all thy ways,
Nor lazy nor contentious days;
And when thy soul and body part,
As innocent as now thou art.

RICHARD CORBET
BISHOP OF NORWICH

She Formed the Habit in
Her Earliest Years

She formed the habit in her earliest years
of coming to my room each morning so
I'd wait for her as you might hope for light.
She'd enter, say hello, take up my pen,
open my books, sit on my bed, disturb
my papers, laugh – then leave abruptly as
a bird that passes. Easier then in mind
I'd take up what she'd interrupted till
among my manuscripts I'd come across
some funny arabesque she'd scribbled or
a few blank pages which she'd crumpled up –
and somehow, though I don't know why, on these
would always come my most successful lines.
She loved our God, loved flowers, stars, green fields –
pure spirit long before she was a woman!
Her eyes mirrored the brightness of her soul.
She'd tend to ask me what I thought of things –
so many radiant winter evenings spent
discussing history or points of language,
four children grouped around my knees, their mother
close by, some friends too chatting near the fire.
I called that being content with little.
And now she's dead. God help me. How could I
be happy when I knew that she was sad?
I was despondent at the gayest ball
If earlier I'd seen shadows in her eyes.

VICTOR HUGO
translated by Harry Guest

Nettles

My son aged three fell in the nettle bed.
'Bed' seemed a curious name for those green spears,
That regiment of spite behind the shed:
It was no place for rest. With sobs and tears
The boy came seeking comfort and I saw
White blisters beaded on his tender skin.
We soothed him till his pain was not so raw.
At last he offered us a watery grin,
And then I took my hook and honed the blade
And went outside and slashed in fury with it
Till not a nettle in that fierce parade
Stood upright anymore. Next task: I lit
A funeral pyre to burn the fallen dead.
But in two weeks the busy sun and rain
Had called up tall recruits behind the shed:
My son would often feel sharp wounds again.

VERNON SCANNELL

A Letter to My Future Child

When, dragging hideous crutches, war
is harrowing your land
and tearing up your country like a rag,
when paddy fields lack days to sprout young shoots
and there's no time for grass to grow,
I'm writing you this letter now
while I've no family yet.
Who will she be, your mother? I don't know.
But I believe you'll come into our world.
You'll enter it not while the curfew's on,
not stillborn and not writhing in an ambulance
like the second child of Aunt and Uncle Vinh,
or like many other children in these times.
Your father hopes you'll come into our world
with robust body and stout limbs.
You'll enter like a rising sun,
the Eastern sun, the summer sun.
You shall grow up amid the sounds of joy.
Along with vast green fields of rice,
along with grass and trees you'll live.
Hearing no plane by day, no gun at nights,
you'll sleep untroubled sleep –
the sleep of radiant innocence.
Each morning, leaving home, I shall kiss you
beside the cradle fragrant with your mother's milk.
On your red lips shall bloom a smile,
a wholesome smile.

The greatest dreams on earth
I trust to you my child.
You are the seed of humankind,
the hope, the future of the world.

TRÁN ĐÚC UYÉN
translated by Huynh Sanh Thong

The Prophet

And a woman who held a babe against her bosom said, Speak to us of Children.

And he said:

Your children are not your children.

They are the sons and daughters of Life's longing for itself.

They come through you but not from you,

And though they are with you yet they belong not to you.

You may give them your love but not your thoughts,

For they have their own thoughts.

You may house their bodies but not their souls,

For their souls dwell in the house of tomorrow, which you cannot visit, not even in your dreams.

You may strive to be like them, but seek not to make them like you.

For life goes not backward nor tarries with yesterday.

KAHLIL GIBRAN

I'll Hold Your Hand

They were unkind steps, no rail for the old and shaken,
And there they lay. Most days, on my way home,
They brought me to a stand – a halting moment;
'If you should fall,' they said, 'if you should fall.'
I was standing there feeling rather fearful and old,
When I heard a voice behind me, a childish voice,
Almost too soft to be heard, and into my hand
A very small hand came, peacefully holding mine.
It was such a small hand, a six year old hand perhaps,
Holding my withered fingers in innocent grasp;
It was matched by the sweetest voice, and the confident message:
'I'll hold your hand till you get down those steps.'
I don't think I could have fallen after that;
It would have been blasphemy to think of falling;
So step by step I went hopefully to the road.
I dared then to look round, but the child had vanished;
I never saw her – but something stirred in me,
Someone had come, someone had come to help me.

MARGARET CROPPER

Seventeenth-century Nun's Prayer

Lord thou knowest better than I know myself that I am growing older and will someday be old. Keep me from the fatal habit of thinking I must say something on every subject and on every occasion. Release me from craving to straighten out everybody's affairs. Make me thoughtful but not moody: helpful but not bossy. With my vast store of wisdom, it seems a pity not to use it all, but thou knowest Lord that I want a few friends at the end.

Keep my mind free from the recital of endless details; give me wings to get to the point. Seal my lips on my aches and pains. They are increasing and love of rehearsing them is becoming sweeter as the years go by. I dare not ask for grace enough to enjoy the tales of others' pains, but help me to endure them with patience.

I dare not ask for improved memory, but for a growing humility and a lessing cocksureness when my memory seems to clash with the memories of others. Teach me the glorious lesson that occasionally I may be mistaken.

Keep me reasonably sweet; I do not want to be a Saint – some of them are so hard to live with – but a sour old person is one of the crowning works of the devil. Give me the ability to see good things in unexpected places, and talents in unexpected people. And, give me, O Lord, the grace to tell them so. Amen.

ANONYMOUS

Song of an Old Woman
Abandoned By Her Tribe

Alas, that I should die,
That I should die now,
I who know so much!

It will miss me,
The twirling fire stick;
The fire coal between the hearth stones,
It will miss me.

The Medicine songs,
The songs of magic healing;
The medicine herbs by the water borders,
They will miss me:
The basket willow,
It will miss me;
All the wisdom of women,
It will miss me.

Alas, that I should die,
Who know so much.

ANONYMOUS
SOUTHERN SOHONE SONG
reworked by Mary Austin

Loveliest of Trees ...

Loveliest of trees, the cherry now
Is hung with bloom along the bough,
And stands about the woodland ride
Wearing white for Eastertide.

Now, of my threescore years and ten,
Twenty will not come again,
And take from seventy springs a score,
It only leaves me fifty more.

And since to look at things in bloom
Fifty springs are little room,
About the woodlands I will go
To see the cherry hung with snow.

A. E. HOUSMAN

➤➤ *6* ◄◄

I believe no pain is lost

UNDERSTANDING CONSOLATION

… rest your life against his song,
It's rest enough for anyone.

I believe no pain is lost

Our programme for Remembrance Day 2000 was called 'An Exacting Joy', a title chosen by Dame Cicely Saunders, founder of St Christopher's Hospice in South London, and pioneer of the modern hospice movement. The words come from a poem by Anne Ridler called 'Christmas and Common Birth': 'To bear new life or learn to live is an exacting joy.' In that programme Dame Cicely spoke from her own personal experience, and that of her patients and their families, of how it is possible, eventually, to wrest new life from the tears and ashes of bereavement.

Something Understood is often about ways of dealing with the most painful times in life with creativity and hope. We try to avoid sentimental and easy answers, Pollyanna brightness and false optimism. We would be honest and realistic about the difficulties and suffering that life brings, and while we recognise that some people suffer far more harrowingly than others we know, too, that no one is immune.

In the first grip of pain or loss, or in the depths of loneliness, guilt or despair, words of comfort and consolation, such as those in this chapter, may only seem to mock the pain. But, later perhaps, they may begin to help, touching our need for comfort or understanding, forgiveness or faith.

Dame Cicely Saunders,
speaking in 'An Exacting Joy'

I've had a lot of joy in my life but it hasn't been easily come by, and the hardest times have brought the best joys; but you have to be ready to be open and to let it happen.

I don't think you help anybody by trying to explain anything at the point of immediate loss. There what they need is the arm round the shoulder, even your own tears, because seeing parting goes on hurting however many times you see it. But what I think is important to realise is that people do make a journey, or *can* make a journey, even though you may go to and fro in a not very straight journey.

I don't think anybody should feel guilty if they find it very difficult; if they find themselves feeling angry or guilty – all sorts of feelings – because I think bereavement can produce very muddled feelings. But I think that if you can hold on to some of the good memories, and go back to them, they grow, and help you to grow.

We're in a world in which love and loss seem to go together and perhaps they have to go together. But it does mean that we can say to God: 'Why did you make it like this?' Yet what has helped me make the journey, and learn more and more along the way, is realising that God is suffering there too: it's the creative suffering of God himself which goes on right through time and eternity. It's not a vengeful God taking it out on you; it's God minding just how you feel.

Father Iain Matthew, Carmelite Friar and writer on St John of the Cross, speaking in 'Dark Night of the Soul'

St John of the Cross's suffering was essential to him becoming who he became, as if his life was being pared down to a fine point that enabled him to speak the word that he was destined to speak. He experienced in prison the stripping of all the layers of protection that would normally allow a person to face into life, as if he was being pushed beyond his own resources. And it was there that he experienced in a way that hadn't been possible before, God's unpaid-for desire to love him.

Throughout his forty-nine years of life he most *lived* when he was taken beyond his own resources. It's exactly here, in this place of darkness, reversal and dysfunction, where everything that made him who he was and sustained him in his journey seemed to be ripped off him – it's in this place that something was released in him which wasn't available before. It's in his imprisonment that he began to compose and later write down the extraordinary poetry for which he is famous, which was born of his being loved at the point where he was weakest.

It's as if his words issue very directly from his experience of darkness and what he came to know there. And that's the extraordinary gift that John offers to the world. He assures me that the darkness in my life is a place in which God can be particularly present, and most directly close.

In the Hour of My Distress

In the hour of my distress,
When temptations me oppress,
And when I my sins confess,
    Sweet Spirit comfort me!

When I lie within my bed,
Sick in heart and sick in head,
And with doubts discomforted,
    Sweet Spirit comfort me!

When the tapers now burn blue,
And the comforters are few,
And that number more than true,
    Sweet Spirit comfort me!

When the Judgment is reveal'd,
And that open'd which was seal'd,
When to Thee I have appeal'd;
    Sweet Spirit, comfort me!

ROBERT HERRICK

On Another's Sorrow

Can I see another's woe,
And not be in sorrow too?
Can I see another's grief,
And not seek for kind relief?

Can I see a falling tear,
And not feel my sorrow's share?
Can a father see his child
Weep, nor be with sorrow fill'd?

Can a mother sit and hear
An infant groan, an infant fear?
No, no! never can it be!
Never, never can it be!

And can he who smiles on all
Hear the wren with sorrows small,
Hear the small bird's grief and care,
Hear the woes that infants bear,

And not sit beside the nest,
Pouring pity in their breast;
And not sit the cradle near,
Weeping tear on infant's tear;

And not sit both night and day,
Wiping all our tears away?
O, no! never can it be!
Never, never can it be!

He doth give his joy to all;
He becomes an infant small;
He becomes a man of woe;
He doth feel the sorrow too.

Think not thou canst sigh a sigh
And thy maker is not by;
Think not thou canst weep a tear,
And thy maker is not near.

O! he gives to us his joy
That our grief he may destroy;
Till our grief is fled and gone
He doth sit by us and moan.

WILLIAM BLAKE

The Dark Night

So dark the night! At rest
and hushed my house, I went with no one knowing
upon a lover's quest
— Ah, the sheer grace! — so blest,
my eager heart with love aflame and glowing.

In darkness, hid from sight
I went by secret ladder safe and sure
— Ah, grace of sheer delight! —
so softly veiled by night,
hushed now my house, in darkness and secure.

Hidden in that glad night,
regarding nothing as I stole away,
no one to see my flight,
no other guide or light
save one that in my heart burned bright as day.

Surer than noonday sun,
guiding me from the start this radiant light
led me to that dear One
waiting for me, well-known,
somewhere apart where no one came in sight.

Dark of the night, my guide,
fairer by far than dawn when stars grow dim!
Night that has unified
the Lover and the Bride,
transforming the Beloved into him.

There on my flowered breast
that none but he might ever own or keep,
he stayed, sinking to rest,
and softly I caressed
my Love while cedars gently fanned his sleep.

Breeze from the turret blew
ruffling his hair. Then with his tranquil hand
wounding my neck, I knew
nothing: my senses flew
at touch of peace too deep to understand.

Forgetting all, my quest
ended, I stayed lost to myself at last.
All ceased: my face was pressed
upon my Love, at rest,
with all my cares among the lilies cast.

ST JOHN OF THE CROSS

Mary Magdalene

She came in deep repentance,
    And knelt down at His feet
Who can change the sorrow into joy,
    The bitter into sweet.

She had cast away her jewels
    And her rich attire,
And her breast was filled with a holy shame,
    And her heart with a holy fire.

Her tears were more precious
    Than her precious pearls –
Her tears that fell upon His feet
    As she wiped them with her curls.

Her youth and her beauty
    Were budding to their prime;
But she wept for the great transgression,
    The sin of other time.

Trembling betwixt hope and fear,
    She sought the King of Heaven,
Forsook the evil of her ways,
    Loved much, and was forgiven.

CHRISTINA GEORGINA ROSSETTI

Love

Love bade me welcome: yet my soul drew back,
        Guiltie of dust and sinne,
But quick-ey'd Love, observing me grow slack
        From my first entrance in,
Drew nearer to me, sweetly questioning
        If I lacked anything.

'A guest,' I answered, 'worthy to be here':
        Love said, 'You shall be he.'
'I, the unkinde, ungratefull? Ah my deare,
        I cannot look on thee.'
Love took my hand, and smiling did reply,
        'Who made the eyes but I?'

'Truth, Lord; but I have marred them: let my shame
        go where it doth deserve.'
'And know you not,' sayes Love, 'who bore the blame?'
        'My deare, then I will serve.'
'You must sit down,' sayes Love, 'and taste my meat.'
        So I did sit and eat.

GEORGE HERBERT

All You Who Sleep Tonight

All you who sleep tonight
Far from the ones you love,
No hand to left or right,
And emptiness above –

Know that you aren't alone.
The whole world shares your tears,
Some for two nights or one,
And some for all their years.

VIKRAM SETH

Shadows

And if tonight my soul may find her peace
in sleep, and sink in good oblivion,
and in the morning wake like a new-opened flower
then I have been dipped again in God, and new-created.

And if, as weeks go round, in the dark of the moon
my spirit darkens and goes out, and soft strange gloom
pervades my movements and my thoughts and words
then I shall know that I am walking still
with God, we are close together now the moon's in shadow.

And if as autumn deepens and darkens
I feel the pain of falling leaves, and stems that break in storms
and trouble and dissolution and distress
and then the softness of deep shadows folding, folding
around my soul and spirit, around my lips
so sweet, like a swoon, or more like the drowse of a low, sad, song
singing darker than the nightingale, on, on to the solstice
and the silence of short days, the silence of the year, the shadow,
with the dark earth, and drenched
with the deep oblivion of earth's lapse and renewal.

And if, in the changing phases of man's life
I fall in sickness and in misery
my wrists seem broken and my heart seems dead
and strength is gone, and my life
is only the leavings of a life:

and still among it all, snatches of lovely oblivion, and snatches
                                    of renewal
odd wintry flowers upon the withered stem, yet new strange
                                    flowers
such as my life has not brought forth before, new blossoms of me —

then I must know that still
I am in the hands of the unknown God,
he is breaking me down to his own oblivion
to send me forth on a new morning, a new man.

D. H. LAWRENCE

I Believe

I believe
no pain is lost.
No tear unmarked,
no cry of anguish
dies unheard,
lost in the hail of gunfire
or blanked out by the padded cell.
I believe that pain
and prayer
are somehow saved,
processed,
stored,
used in the Divine Economy.
The blood
shed in Salvador
will irrigate the heart
of some financier
a million miles away.
The terror,
pain,
despair,
swamped
by lava, flood or earthquake
will be caught up
like mist and fall again,
a gentle rain
on arid hearts
or souls despairing
in the back streets
of Brooklyn.

SHEILA CASSIDY

Extreme Unction

Upon the eyes, the lips, the feet,
    On all the passages of sense,
The atoning oil is spread with sweet
    Renewal of lost innocence.

The feet, that lately ran so fast
    To meet desire, are soothly sealed;
The eyes, that were so often cast
    On vanity, are touched and healed.

From troublous sights and sounds set free;
    In such a twilight hour of breath,
Shall one retrace his life, or see,
    Through shadows, the true face of death?

Vials of mercy! Sacring oils!
    I know not whence nor when I come,
Nor through what wanderings and toils,
    To crave of you Viaticum.

Yet, when the walls of flesh grow weak,
    In such an hour, it well may be,
Through mist and darkness, light will break,
    And each anointed sense will see.

ERNEST DOWSON

Farewell

Farewell to Thee! But not farewell
To all my fondest thoughts of Thee;
Within my heart they still shall dwell
And they shall cheer and comfort me.

Life seems more sweet that Thou didst live
And men more true that Thou wert one;
Nothing is lost that Thou didst give,
Nothing destroyed that Thou hast done.

ANNE BRONTË

After Frost

It's hard to tell what bird it is
Singing in the misty wood,
Or the reason for its song
So late after evening's come.

When all else has dropped its name
Down into the scented dark
Its song grown cool and clear says
Nothing much to anyone.

But catches hold a whisper in my brain
That only now is understood.
It says, rest your life against his song,
It's rest enough for anyone.

BRIAN PATTEN

7

Good luck? Bad luck? Who knows?

UNDERSTANDING HARD TIMES

Are you willing to be made nothing?
dipped into oblivion?

If not, you will never really change.

Good luck? Bad luck? Who knows?

Not all of life's hard times are quite as hard as those in the last chapter. Often they are disappointing rather than devastating, confusing rather than crushing. But still such times can undermine our joy and confidence, make us anxious, fretful and distracted, and drain our days of colour. Sometimes, in these circumstances, it helps to be nudged into a different way of seeing the situation. Some kind but robust insight from a friend or observer can transform our understanding of what we are going through and in doing so bring a return of energy and hope.

The writings here do just that: from the ancient wisdom of Chinese folk tales and the modern wisdom of the Vietnamese Buddhist Thich Nhat Hanh, to the laconic advice of Sydney Smith and Jeremy Taylor, they offer some different thoughts and perspectives on the things which happen to us and the difficult situations in which we find ourselves. Then, finally, in D. H. Lawrence's 'Phoenix' there is the more stern reminder that the cycle of darkness and light, death and rebirth, is essential to all life and change and growth, not least to our own.

Philip Sheldrake, speaking in 'Changes and Chances'

I don't think that we will ever fully grasp who or what God is. There is always a mystery in God; there is always something that is leading us onward beyond the images of God that we have. But I think that at the heart of the Christian faith is certainly a sense of the *stability* of God, and of God's irrevocable commitment to the created order: to me as an individual and to humanity as a whole. And in that sense, God is not fickle; God does not become unreliable. So, while there's a way in which we can sometimes turn the notion of the 'changelessness' of God into something static and fixed, I don't believe that's the Christian faith. The changelessness of God that I understand to be at the heart of Christianity is much more to do with our sense of God's utter reliability.

Good Luck? Bad Luck? Who Knows?

There is a Chinese story of an old farmer who had an old horse for tilling his fields. One day the horse escaped into the hills and when all the farmer's neighbours sympathised with the old man over his bad luck, the farmer replied, 'Bad luck? Good luck? Who knows?' A week later the horse returned with a herd of wild horses from the hills and this time the neighbours congratulated the farmer on his good luck. His reply was, 'Good luck? Bad luck? Who knows?' Then when the farmer's son was attempting to tame one of the wild horses, he fell off its back and broke his leg. Everyone thought this very bad luck. Not the farmer, whose only reaction was, 'Bad luck? Good luck? Who knows?' Some weeks later the army marched into the village and conscripted every able-bodied youth they found there. When they saw the farmer's son with his broken leg they let him off. Now was that good luck? Bad luck? Who knows?

Everything that seems on the surface to be an evil may be a good in disguise. And everything that seems good on the surface may really be an evil. So we are wise when we leave it to God to decide what is good luck and what bad, and thank him that all things turn out for good with those who love him.

RETOLD BY ANTHONY DE MELLO

The Power in Needing Less

Which is dearer,
    Name or life?
Which means more,
    Life or wealth?
Which is worse,
    Gain or loss?

The stronger the attachments,
    The greater the cost.
The more that is hoarded,
    The deeper the loss.

Know what is enough;
    Be without disgrace.
Know when to stop;
    Be without danger.

In this way one lasts for a very long time.

LAO TZU
translated by R. L. Wing

Hope as an Obstacle

Western civilisation places so much emphasis on the idea of hope that we sacrifice the present moment. Hope is for the future. It cannot help us discover joy, peace, or enlightenment in the present moment. Many religions are based on the notion of hope, and this teaching about refraining from hope may create a strong reaction. But the shock can bring about something important. I do not mean that you should not have hope, but that hope is not enough. Hope can create an obstacle for you, and if you dwell in the energy of hope, you will not bring yourself back entirely into the present moment. If you re-channel those energies into being aware of what is going on in the present moment, you will be able to make a breakthrough and discover joy and peace right in the present moment, inside of yourself and all around you.

THICH NHAT HANH

Contentedness

Enjoy the present whatsoever it be, and be not solicitous for the future; for if you take your foot from the present standing, and thrust it forward towards tomorrow's event, you are in a restless condition; it is like refusing to quench your present thirst, by fearing you shall want drink the next day. If it be well today, it is madness to make the present miserable by fearing it may be ill tomorrow; when your belly is full of today's dinner, to fear you shall want the next day's supper: for it may be you shall not, and then to what purpose was this day's affliction? But if tomorrow you shall want, your sorrow will come time enough though you do not hasten it; let your trouble tarry till its own day comes. But if it chance to be ill today, do not increase it by the care of tomorrow: enjoy the blessings of this day, if God sends them, and the evils of it bear patiently and sweetly: for this day is only ours; we are dead to yesterday, and we are not yet born to the morrow.

JEREMY TAYLOR

Advice on Low Spirits

Nobody has suffered more from low spirits than I have done, so I feel for you.

1. Live as well and drink as much wine as you dare. 2. Go in to the shower-bath with a small quantity of water at a temperature low enough to give you a *slight* sensation of cold – 75 or 80°. 3. Amusing books. 4. Short views of human life not farther than dinner or tea. 5. Be as busy as you can. 6. See as much as you can of those friends who respect and like you; 7. and of those acquaintances who amuse you. 8. Make no secret of low spirits to your friends but talk of them fully: they are always the worse for dignified concealment. 9. Attend to the effects tea and coffee produce upon you. 10. Compare your lot with that of other people. 11. Don't expect too much of human life, a sorry business at best. 12. Avoid poetry, dramatic representations (except comedy), music, serious novels, melancholy sentimental people, and everything likely to excite feeling or emotion not ending in active benevolence. 13. Do good and endeavour to please everybody of every degree. 14. Be as much as you can in the open air without fatigue. 15. Make the room where you commonly sit gay and pleasant. 16. Struggle little by little against idleness. 17. Don't be too severe upon yourself, but do yourself justice. 18. Keep good, blazing fires. 19. Be firm and constant in the exercise of rational religion. 20. Believe me dear Lady Georgiana very truly yours, SYDNEY SMITH.

SYDNEY SMITH

At Parting

Since we through war awhile must part
Sweetheart, and learn to lose
Daily use
Of all that satisfied our heart:
Lay up those secrets and those powers
Wherewith you pleased and cherished me these two years.

Now we must draw, as plants would,
On tubers stored in a better season,
Our honey and heaven;
Only our love can store such food.
Is this to make a god of absence?
A new-born monster to steal our sustenance?

We cannot quite cast out lack and pain.
Let him remain – what he may devour
We can well spare:
He never can tap this, the true vein.
I have no words to tell you what you were,
But when you are sad, think, Heaven could give no more.

ANNE RIDLER

Phoenix

Are you willing to be sponged out, erased, cancelled,
made nothing?
Are you willing to be made nothing?
dipped into oblivion?

If not, you will never really change.

The phoenix renews her youth
only when she is burnt, burnt alive, burnt down
to hot and flocculent ash.
Then the small stirring of a new small bub in the nest
with strands of down like floating ash
shows that she is renewing her youth like the eagle,
immortal bird.

D. H. LAWRENCE

8

And every common bush
afire with God

UNDERSTANDING A DEEPER REALITY

I see for one crammed second, order so
Explicit that I need no more persuasion.

And every common bush afire with God

In the Preface to this collection I said that 'God is a given' in the making of Something Understood. *The spiritual dimension of life, however variously understood, is acknowledged as both real and important, even in those programmes with the most secular-sounding titles.*

Some people have a constant sense of this other dimension, underpinning all life and present in all creation. Elizabeth Barrett Browning writes of such a vision in 'Aurora Leigh', as does Walt Whitman in 'Miracles':

> As to me I know of nothing else but miracles,
> Whether I walk the streets of Manhattan,
> Or dart my sight over the roofs of houses toward the sky.

For most others, however, such awareness comes in fleeting glimpses, moments suspended in time, chinks of light: when the veil is drawn back and that deeper reality breaks in upon our consciousness. So Elizabeth Jennings can write of the transforming impact of 'one crammed second', Sri Aurobindo, of a heavenly shadow in the farthest corner of his eye, and Nayana Jani of a 'soundless explosion', which only those without ears can hear.

Kathleen Raine, the poet, speaking in 'The Sacred'

William Blake was very close to the Vedic teaching that what he called 'the divine humanity' is the divine presence in everyone, and to Blake that living divine presence in us is our reality and not our physical bodies, which he called 'the garment not the man'. In India of course the sacred is just in the air one breathes, while in this country it's very far from being in the air one breathes. In fact the materialist ideologies of the West almost preclude the experience of the sacred; they cut us off from it. They expect us to know things by observation of an external object and they try to measure dreams by putting electrodes on the head of the dreamer. But that does not tell one the dream. That may measure something else, but it is the dream itself that is the sacred experience.

Angela Tilby, television producer, lecturer and Anglican priest, speaking in 'Science and Faith'

Quantum mechanics is one of those things which has emerged this century in science and it's really about how matter behaves at the sub-atomic level. That's beyond the point at which you can see it or touch it or feel it. It's the invisible aspect of matter, and what you find is that it doesn't behave in predictable, organised ways – in the way that Newton, with his great laws of motion, predicted that it would.

Now why this is terribly important is that it shows that at this more basic level of organisation there's a certain amount of chance built into the universe: a certain amount of fluidity and flexibility, even a sort of freedom about matter which we wouldn't have guessed at if we only had Newton's physics to go on.

Extrapolating from the science, what this undermines is the idea that, if there is a God, he has got everything planned from the very first moment of creation until the very last moment, when it's all wound up. That sort of relentless Calvinism, where every single motion in the universe is predictable becomes impossible if there is a degree of freedom in the way the universe is unfolding: a freedom which requires a sort of response.

When I first learnt about quantum physics I thought this is absolutely wonderful because it frees me from all kinds of hang-ups about the inexorable will of God, and it suggests that the universe has a part to play in building itself under God's guidance. That God in a way asks the universe a question which we then have to answer as conscious beings. This is an evolving universe: it's not a place where the answer is laid out in the question. Because the universe is so open I find it much easier to believe in a God who might actually care what happens to it.

Aurora Leigh

But man, the twofold creature, apprehends
The twofold manner, in and outwardly,
And nothing in the world comes single to him ...

           ... 'There's nothing great
Nor small,' has said a poet of our day,
Whose voice will ring beyond the curfew of eve
And not be thrown out by the matin's bell:
And truly, I reiterate, nothing's small!
No lily-muffled hum of a summer bee,
But finds some coupling with the spinning stars;
Nor pebble at your foot, but proves a sphere;
No chaffinch, but implies the cherubim;
And (glancing on my own thin, veinèd wrist)
In such a little tremor of the blood
The whole strong clamour of a vehement soul
Doth utter itself distinct. Earth's crammed with heaven,
And every common bush afire with God;
But only he who sees, takes off his shoes,
The rest sit round it and pluck blackberries,
And daub their natural faces unaware
More and more from the first similitude.

ELIZABETH BARRETT BROWNING

On the Beach at Night Alone

On the beach at night alone,
As the old mother sways her to and fro singing her husky song,
As I watch the bright stars shining, I think a thought of the clef
      of the universes and of the future.

A vast similitude interlocks all,
All spheres, grown, ungrown, small, large, suns, moons, planets,
All distances of place however wide,
All distances of time, all inanimate forms,
All souls, all living bodies though they be ever so different,
      or in different worlds,
All gaseous, watery, vegetable, mineral processes, the fishes,
      the brutes,
All nations, colours, barbarisms, civilisations, languages,
All identities that have existed or may exist on this globe,
      or any globe,
All lives and deaths, all of the past, present, future,
This vast similitude spans them, and always has spann'd,
And shall forever span them and compactly hold and enclose
      them.

WALT WHITMAN

Miracles

Why, who makes much of a miracle?
As to me I know nothing else but miracles,
Whether I walk the streets of Manhattan,
Or dart my sight over the roofs of houses toward the sky,
Or wade with naked feet along the beach just in the edge of the
   water,
Or stand under trees in the woods,
Or talk by day with any one I love, or sleep in the bed at night
   with any one I love,
Or sit at table at dinner with the rest,
Or look at strangers opposite me riding in the car,
Or watch honey-bees busy around the hive of a summer
   forenoon,
Or animals feeding in the fields,
Or birds, or the wonderfulness of insects in the air,
Or the wonderfulness of the sundown, or of stars shining so
   quiet and bright,
Or the exquisite delicate thin curve of the new moon in spring;
These with the rest, one and all, are to me miracles,
The whole referring, yet each distinct and in its place.

To me every hour of the light and dark is a miracle,
Every cubic inch of space is a miracle,
Every square yard of the surface of the earth is spread with
   the same,
Every foot of the interior swarms with the same.

To me the sea is a continual miracle,
The fishes that swim — the rocks — the motion of the waves —
   the ships with men in them.
What stranger miracles are there?

WALT WHITMAN

The World As I See It

The fairest thing we can experience is the mysterious. It is the fundamental emotion which stands at the cradle of true art and true science. He who knows it not and can no longer wonder, no longer feel amazement, is as good as dead, a snuffed-out candle. It was the experience of mystery – even if mixed with fear – that engendered religion. A knowledge of the existence of something we cannot penetrate, of the manifestations of the profoundest reason and the most radiant beauty, which are only accessible to our reason in their most elementary forms – it is this knowledge and this emotion that constitute the truly religious attitude; in this sense, and in this alone, I am a deeply religious man.

ALBERT EINSTEIN

You Never Enjoy the World Aright ...

You never enjoy the world aright, till the sea itself floweth in your veins, till you are clothed with the heavens, and crowned with the stars: and perceive yourself to be the sole heir of the whole world, and more than so, because men are in it who are every one sole heirs as well as you. Till you can sing and rejoice and delight in God, as misers do in gold, and Kings in sceptres, you never enjoy the world.

THOMAS TRAHERNE

Hermitage at Broken-Hill Monastery

Within this convent old
By the clear dawn
Tall woods are lit with earliest rays.
Lo here and there a pathway strays
On to a hidden lawn
Whose flowery thickets cells enfold.

The light upon yon hill
Lulls every bird;
And shadows on dark tarns set free
The souls of men from vanity.
Each sound of earth is still
Only the temple bell is heard.

CH'ANG CHIEN
translated by John Turner

This Was the Moment

From: BC:AD

This was the moment when Before
Turned into After, and the future's
Uninvented timekeepers presented arms.

This was the moment when nothing
Happened. Only dull peace
Sprawled boringly over the earth.

This was the moment when even energetic Romans
Could find nothing better to do
Than counting heads in remote provinces.

And this was the moment
When a few farm workers and three
Members of an obscure Persian sect
Walked haphazardly by starlight straight
Into the kingdom of heaven.

U. A. FANTHORPE

I Count the Moments

I count the moments of my mercies up,
I make a list of love and find it full.
I do all this before I fall asleep.

Others examine consciences. I tell
My beads of gracious moments shining still.
I count my good hours and they guide me well

Into a sleepless night. It's when I fill
Pages with what I think I am made for,
A life of writing poems. Then may they heal

The pain of silence for all those who stare
At stars as I do but are helpless to
Make the bright necklace. May I set ajar

The doors of closed minds. Words come and words go
And poetry is pain as well as passion.
But in the large flights of imagination

I see for one crammed second, order so
Explicit I need no more persuasion.

ELIZABETH JENNINGS

Revelation

Someone leaping from the rocks
Past me ran with wind-blown locks
Like a startled bright surmise
Visible to mortal eyes, –
Just a cheek of frightened rose
That with sudden beauty glows,
Just a footstep like the wind
And a hurried glance behind,
And then nothing, – as a thought
Escapes the mind ere it is caught.
Someone of the heavenly rout
From behind the veil ran out.

SRI AUROBINDO

The Soundless Explosion

Something breaks and cracks, merges with something else
Whatever once was made of gold, again melts into a lump
of gold.

The mountains are submerged, the oceans surge
Then azure sky turns wet and crouches down in the showers.
Nothing can be found where it once was.
All forts and castles come crashing down in this upheaval.
Even that which was collected and preserved for endless births
melts, loses shape.

Existence itself dissolves into an elixir.
In the soundless explosion of this moment
Only those who without ears can listen, hear it.

NAYANA JANI
edited by Arlene Zide and Bharat Pathak

9

God of all the opposites

UNDERSTANDING TENSION AND PARADOX

I prayed to God for safety – to tread the trodden path;
I was granted danger, to lose track and find the Way.

God of all the opposites

Faith can raise far more questions than it answers. Despite, or perhaps in part because of, our advancing knowledge and technological invent-iveness, the world remains a puzzling place; and puzzles challenge faith. So many issues do not lend themselves to neat solutions; so many different opinions need to be weighed; so many different causes shout for our attention; so many tensions and conflicts leave us strug-gling in their net. And in the face of such confusion faith does not always seem to work as we believe it should: it does not often smooth the path or stop the pain, give us the answer or fix things quick.

The readings in this chapter touch realistically on some of the ten-sions and paradoxes that we are forced to confront: science and faith, orthodoxy and renewal, 'metaphor and dogma', withdrawal from the world and involvement in it. But beyond the tension and confusion they too point to that deep, underlying reality we spoke of in the last chapter, the Laughing Love of John Hemming's 'God of All the Opposites', that holds all things together, in Love's hand.

David Scott, poet and Anglican priest, speaking in 'Impossible Prayer'

I believe that God, at heart, is longing for peace in the world, and the question why he doesn't produce peace out of a hat must depend on the sort of constraints that his love and desire for peace are under. Traditionally, these constraints have been understood as something to do with his desire to give us autonomy, free will; the desire to allow us to grow up and to make mistakes. But within these constraints he longs for peace from us and for us.

The best image of the limitations of God that I know is in Christ himself. Christ intervened – or intervenes – and when he most vividly intervened he did so as a human being. If we look at Christ, the constraints that we see are the inevitability of suffering, because love involves suffering, and that if we're going to have a world where we have the power to love we also have the power to hate. And that's the world in which we actually live. We haven't got a perfect world; we haven't got a paradise; we've got a mixture, and that is itself a wonderful thing because it means we have the *ability* to believe: we're not constrained to believe, and we also have the ability to be self-sacrificial.

The Burning Bush

When Moses, musing in the desert, found
The thorn bush spiking up from the hot ground,
And saw the branches, on a sudden, bear
The crackling yellow barberries of fire,

He searched his learning and imagination
For any logical, neat explanation,
And turned to go, but turned again and stayed
And faced the fire and knew it for his God.

I too have seen the briar alight like coal,
The love that burns, the flesh that's ever whole,
And many times have turned and left it there,
Saying: 'It's prophecy – but metaphor.'

But stinging tongues like John the Baptist shout:
'That this is metaphor is no way out.
It's dogma too, or you make God a liar;
The bush is still a bush, and fire is fire.'

NORMAN NICHOLSON

God, Chance and Necessity

Really to believe in God is to have some experience of a being of transcendent power and value which is life-enhancing and value-transforming, and to trust the testimony of at least some of those who claim such experience to a pre-eminent degree. It is to experience a mystery beyond human comprehension, which sets limits to all human understanding, unless and insofar as it is empowered by the divine itself. Such an experience neither biology nor philosophy, nor indeed theology, can bring about. It may be, however, that the intelligible goal of the whole cosmic process is an entrance into the 'instructed ignorance' of love that lies beyond all proud claims to the omnipotence of human reason. There is no conflict between reason, the deepest understanding of the cosmos, and faith, the trusting response to the mystery of divine love. Together, they express the commitment to truth that should be the hallmark of science and the humility that should be the hallmark of faith. Only reason and faith together can bring humans and all sentient creatures to that maturity that is their proper form of life. Only then can the universe achieve that fully conscious relationship to its creator in which its created potentialities for good can find their proper fulfilment. That is the ultimate purpose of God and the goal of evolution.

KEITH WARD

Narziss and Goldmund

Seen from above – as God might see it – were this patterned order and morality, this giving up of the world, and the joys of sense, this aloof withdrawal from blood and mire into prayer and philosophy, any better? Were men really made to live an ordered life, its virtues and duties set to the ringing of a bell? Was man created to study Aristotle and the *Summa*, to know Greek, extinguish his senses, fly the world? Had not God made man with lusts and pride in him, with blood and darkness in his heart, with the freedom to sin, love and despair? Whenever Narziss thought of Goldmund such questions were foremost in his mind.

Yes, and perhaps it was not merely simpler and more human to live a Goldmund-life in the world. Perhaps in the end it was more valiant, and greater in God's sight, to breast the currents of reality, sin, and accept sin's bitter consequence, instead of standing apart, with well-washed hands, living in sober, quiet security, planning a pretty garden of well-trained thoughts, and walking then, in stainless ignorance, among them – the sheltered beds of a little paradise. It was harder perhaps, and needed a stouter heart to walk with broken shoes through forest-glades, to trudge the roads, suffer rain and snow, want and drought, playing all the games of the senses, and paying one's losses with much grief.

HERMANN HESSE

The Passing of Arthur

I found Him in the shining of the stars,
I marked Him in the flowering of His fields,
But in His ways with men I find Him not.
I waged His wars and now I pass and die.
O me! For why is all around us here
As if some lesser God had made the world,
But had not force to shape it as He would,
Till the High God behold it from beyond,
And enter it and make it beautiful?
Or else as if the world were wholly fair,
But that these eyes of men are dense and dim,
And have not power to see it as it is:
Perchance because we see not to the close; –
For I, being simple, thought to work His will,
And have but stricken with the sword in vain;
And all whereon I leaned in wife and friend
Is traitor to my peace, and all my realm
Reels back into the beast, and is no more.
My God, thou hast forgotten me in my death:
Nay – God, my Christ – I pass but shall not die.

ALFRED, LORD TENNYSON

The Law

My grandfather's mind was a covered ark
with doors that sprang shut when the truth was in.
'Pines bend with winds that snap oak.
They stand who bend before God.'

Curtains and an ornamental lock
can light the law, as black soil shines at night;
dazzled by that law, I stood in wonder,
and trembled in the shadow of his hands.

Standing beside him in the synagogue,
I turned and saw a cage of women's faces –
fish leaping in nets – and one of them
my face, when I grew higher than his shoulder.

Stained glass grew leaves of light across the floor;
I saw a various truth with radiant shadows:
'Fathers, forgive me. I cannot follow.'

GRACE SCHULMAN

Penelope and Odysseus as One Person

One wants the world. The wing of dawn
beats in him. More! More!
The other never stirs from the loom.
An ancient rhythm repeats:
'Less – Less –
the real travelling is inward.'

One asks why rest –
the horrible gallop of minutes
will trample us if we stay.
The other stops to caress
A single plume of grass;
leans to petals glistening with rain.

One craves extravagant words,
says to a lover, 'Enchant me.'
The other thread by thread
makes beauty more naked;
slices off a shiver of sunlight,
weighs the moon in a fisherman's net.

One loves storms and clouds,
says death is a skyless country.
The other prefers trees,
says death is a cloud of leaves
where at last we understand
the sayings of the wind.

A shroud of memory grows
between the two of them,
a tapestry of tides and tales.
One is the wave,
the other is the shore:
an endless sea – a story of return.

IOANNA-VERONIKA WARWICK

I Asked for Knowledge

I asked for knowledge – power to control things;
I was granted understanding – to learn to love persons.

I asked for strength to be a Great Man;
I was made weak to become a better Man.

I asked for wealth to make friends;
I became poor, to keep friends.

I asked for all things to enjoy life;
I was granted all life, to enjoy things.

I cried for Pity; I was offered Sympathy.

I craved for healing of my own disorders;
I received insight into another's suffering.

I prayed to God for safety – to tread the trodden path;
I was granted danger, to lose track and find the Way.

I got nothing that I prayed for;
I am among all men, richly blessed.

ANONYMOUS

God of All the Opposites

'O God of All the Opposites,
Is it really True,
If I conjoin all opposites,
I'll think and feel like You?'

'O can I think and feel like You?
And can this really mean
I may BE all the opposites,
As You have ever been?

'O God of All the opposites,
If I can BE True Love,
Shall I be free of opposites
Below Here as Above?

'O God of All the opposites,
Will I really find, –
If I can join All opposites –
WHoly Peace of Mind?

'Shall I find wHoly Peace of Mind,
Shall I be wHoly Whole,
When I can BE my opposites
And See from either pole?

'Will Earth be Heaven and Heaven be Earth?
Will Night be always Day?
Will Black be White and Death be Birth?
And round the opposite way?

'O God of All the opposites,
Pray tell me is this so?'
Says God with wholly Holy Love,
'The answer's Yes … and No.'

WHoly Cross I shout at this,
'AM I SUPPOSED TO GUESS?'
Says Laughing Love, 'The answer is –
Precisely No! … and Yes!'

JOHN HEMMING

＋＋ **10** ＋＋

Walk out with me

UNDERSTANDING THE JOURNEY

... we must go
Though we do not know
Who called, or what marks we shall leave upon the snow.

Walk out with me

'Journeying', 'Travel', 'Pilgrimage', 'A Great Adventure', 'The Hero's Journey', 'Breaking Away', 'Maps', 'Directions', 'None to Accompany Me' ... Ever since Something Understood *began, the Journey is a theme we have returned to again and again. As a commonplace but enduring metaphor for our circuitous and boulder-strewn path through life, the Journey is about risk and discovery, call and response, loss and transformation. It embraces and entwines our inner and outer reality, the spiritual and the physical, the solitary and the shared.*

In 'Safety and Risk' we quoted the French novelist André Gide: 'One does not discover new lands without consenting to lose sight of the shore for a very long time.' It is this sense of launching out purposefully into the unknown, of relinquishing consciously and willingly the security and comfort of the familiar, that informs most of the readings in this chapter. The Journey is undertaken in response to some inner stirring: a 'fire' or 'flame' within, the call of 'a glimmering girl', 'a bright or dark angel'. The outcome is uncertain, the destination unknown; the way may be 'long and weary' and 'uphill to the very end'. It demands perseverance and discernment, and an honest, often humbling, confrontation with our true selves. But what drives the traveller on is a compelling commitment to integrity, and the vision of a future delineated by faith.

Nicholas Luard, speaking in
'Spirit and Place'

In the case of the pilgrimage to Santiago de Compostella the journey and the destination, in a sense, become one, because you're aware throughout – and it's nearly a thousand miles – of the countless people who've been before you. You see the chapels and monasteries, and the convents and the ancient hospitals, and you're constantly aware of pilgrimage. And of course, when you arrive, it's a very defining moment in your life.

... From very early in my childhood, I've been aware of certain places, which have a quality that is almost indefinable. I grew up on the Isle of Mull, and one of my first memories – and the experience has been the same whenever I've made the journey back – is of the Holy Island of Iona which lies just off Mull. It's impossible to put into words but there is no doubt as you take that little sea crossing and approach the little island, lying a bit like a whale in the sea, that you are arriving at somewhere extraordinary, special, different ...

William Dalrymple, speaking in 'Travel'

People ask, 'Why do you travel? Why have you got this wander-lust?', but I always think that man is a travelling animal. Bruce Chatwin was a great believer that man, homo sapiens, has been around in his present form for 100,000 years, and of that, for 95,000 years he was a nomad. Evolution designed us to travel, and Chatwin believed we had in us the urge to migrate seasonally, every bit as much as terns and swifts do: that man is essentially a migratory animal, and that all the troubles of the world – the wars and the tensions and the aggressions of man – come from the suppression of that travelling urge, from being locked up in the walls of a city. There's a lovely quote of Pascal, which I think is very true: 'Our nature lies in movement, complete calm is death.'

The Song of the Wandering Aengus

I went out to the hazel wood,
Because a fire was in my head,
And cut and peeled a hazel wand,
And hooked a berry to a thread;
And when white moths were on the wing
And moth-like stars were flickering out,
I dropped the berry in a stream
And caught a little silver trout.

When I had laid it on the floor
I went to blow the fire aflame,
But something rustled on the floor,
And someone called me by my name:
It had become a glimmering girl
With apple blossom in her hair
Who called me by my name and ran
And faded through the brightening air.

Though I am old with wandering
Through hollow lands and hilly lands,
I will find out where she has gone,
And kiss her lips and take her hands;
And walk among long dappled grass,
And pluck till time and times are done
The silver apples of the moon,
The golden apples of the sun.

W. B. YEATS

The Call

From our low seat beside the fire
    Where we have dozed and dreamed and watched the glow
  Or raked the ashes, stopping so
We scarcely saw the sun or rain
  Above, or looked much higher
Than this same quiet red or burned-out fire.
       To-night we heard a call,
       A rattle on the window-pane,
       A voice on the sharp air,
And felt a breath stirring our hair,
  A flame within us: something swift and tall
  Swept in and out and that was all.
Was it a bright or a dark angel? Who can know?
  It left no mark upon the snow,
    But suddenly it snapped the chain
    Unbarred, flung wide the door
    Which will not shut again;
And so we cannot sit here any more.
       We must arise and go:
       The world is cold without
       And dark and hedged about
       With mystery and enmity and doubt,
       But we must go
       Though we do not know
Who called, or what marks we shall leave upon the snow.

CHARLOTTE MEW

The Pilgrimage

I travell'd on, seeing the hill, where lay
    My expectation.
  A long it was and weary way.
  The gloomy cave of Desperation
I left on th'one, and on the other side
    The rock of Pride.

And so I came to Fancies medow strow'd
    With many a flower:
  Fain would I here have made abode,
  But I was quicken'd by my houre.
So to Cares cops I came, and there got through
    With much ado.

That led me to the wilde of Passion, which
    Some call the wold;
  A wasted place, but sometimes rich.
  Here I was robb'd of all my gold,
Save one good Angell, which a friend had ti'd
    Close to my side.

At length I got unto the gladsome hill
    Where lay my hope,
  Where lay my heart; and climbing still,
  When I had gain'd the brow and top,
A lake of brackish waters on the ground
    Was all I found.

With that abash'd and struck with many a sting
        Of swarming fears,
    I fell and cry'd, Alas my king!
    Can both the way and end be tears?
Yet taking heart I rose, and then perceiv'd
        I was deceiv'd:

My hill was further: so I flung away,
        Yet heard a crie
    Just as I went, *None goes that way*
    And lives: If that be all, said I,
After so foul a journey death is fair,
        And but a chair.

GEORGE HERBERT

Uphill

Does the road wind uphill all the way?
  Yes, to the very end.
Will the day's journey take the whole long day?
  From morn to night, my friend.

But is there for the night a resting-place?
  A roof for when the slow dark hours begin.
May not the darkness hide it from my face?
  You cannot miss that inn.

Shall I meet other wayfarers at night?
  Those who have gone before.
Then must I knock, or call when just in sight?
  They will not keep you standing at that door.

Shall I find comfort, travel-sore and weak?
  Of labour you shall find the sum.
Will there be beds for me and all who seek?
  Yea, beds for all who come.

CHRISTINA GEORGINA ROSSETTI

Passing Through ...

The life of man on earth, my lord, in comparison with the vast stretches of time about which we know nothing, seems to me to resemble the flight of a sparrow, who enters through a window in the great hall warmed by a blazing fire laid in the centre of it, where you feast with your councillors and liègemen, while outside the tempests and snows of winter rage. And the bird swiftly sweeps through the great hall and goes out the other side, and after this brief respite from winter, he goes back into winter and is lost to your eyes. Such is the brief life of man, of which we know neither what goes before nor what comes after ...

THE VENERABLE BEDE

Ozymandias

I met a traveller from an antique land
Who said: Two vast and trunkless legs of stone
Stand in the desert. Near them, on the sand,
Half sunk, a shattered visage lies, whose frown,
And wrinkled lip, and sneer of cold command,
Tell that its sculptor well those passions read
Which yet survive, stamped on these lifeless things,
The hand that mocked them, and the heart that fed;
And on the pedestal these words appear:
'My name is Ozymandias, king of kings:
Look on my works, ye Mighty, and despair!'
Nothing beside remains. Round the decay
Of that colossal wreck, boundless and bare
The lone and level sands stretch far away.

PERCY BYSSHE SHELLEY

Darest Thou Now O Soul

Darest thou now O soul,
Walk out with me toward the
    unknown region,
Where neither ground is for the feet
    nor any path to follow?

No map there, nor guide,
Nor voice sounding, nor touch of
    human hand,
Nor face with blooming flesh, nor
    lips, nor eyes are in that land.

I know it not O soul,
Nor dost thou, all is a blank before us,
All waits undreamed of in that
    region, that inaccessible land.

Till when the ties loosen,
All but the ties eternal, time and space,
Nor darkness, gravitation, sense, nor
    any bounds bounding us.

Then we burst forth, we float,
In time and space O soul, prepared
    for them,
Equal, equipt at last, (O joy! O fruit
    of all!) them to fulfil O soul.

WALT WHITMAN

The Road Not Taken

Two roads diverged in a yellow wood,
And sorry I could not travel both
And be one traveler, long I stood
And looked down one as far as I could
To where it bent in the undergrowth;

Then took the other, as just as fair,
And having perhaps the better claim,
Because it was grassy and wanted wear;
Though as for that the passing there
Had worn them really about the same,

And both that morning equally lay
In leaves no step had trodden black.
Oh, I kept the first for another day!
Yet knowing how way leads on to way,
I doubted if I should ever come back.

I shall be telling this with a sigh
Somewhere ages and ages hence:
Two roads diverged in a wood and I –
I took the one less traveled by
And that has made all the difference.

ROBERT FROST

The Highway

It seems too enormous just for a man to be
Walking on. As if it and the empty day
Were all there is. And a little dog
Trotting in time with the heat waves, off
Near the horizon, seeming never to get
Any farther. The sun and everything
Are stuck in the same places, and the ditch
Is the same all the time, full of every kind
Of bone, while the empty air keeps humming
That sound it has memorized of things going
Past. And the signs with huge heads and starved
Bodies, doing dances in the heat,
And the others big as houses, all promise
But with nothing inside and only one wall,
Tell of other places where you can eat
Drink, get a bath, lie on a bed
Listening to music, and be safe. If you
Look around you see it is just the same
The other way, going back; and farther
Now to where you came from, probably,
Than to places you can reach by going on.

W. S. MERWIN

Journeys

The deception of platforms
where the arrivals and the departures
coincide. And the smiles
on the faces of those welcoming

and bidding farewell are
to conceal the knowledge
that destinations are the familiarities
from which the traveller must set out.

R. S. THOMAS

Map of the New World

I Archipelagoes

At the end of this sentence, rain will begin.
At the rain's edge, a sail.

Slowly the sail will lose sight of islands;
into the mist will go the belief in harbours
of an entire race.

The ten-years' war is finished.
Helen's hair, a grey cloud.
Troy, a white ashpit
by the drizzling sea.

The drizzle tightens like the strings of a harp.
A man with clouded eyes picks up the rain
And plucks the first line of the *Odyssey*.

DEREK WALCOTT

The Commission given to 'Flying Horse' by the Mystic Medicine Chief 'Silver Bear'

When you walk in darkness
It is no use carrying a lantern
Whose light cannot be seen.
For, then, every step you take
Will be a hesitation into the unknown
Where any tiny pebble on the Path
May cause you to trip or stumble,
Or the slightest impediment,
A cause for you to give up
And abandon the journey
To try, perhaps, another path.
So make a lantern
Lit from the Red Indian fire
And whose light shines clear
For the way you've come
To be seen and marked,
And the way ahead to hold no fear
For others who come after you
To walk with an assurance,
Seeing by light from a torch you have left.
For those who walk this Path
Should not be left to grope in the dark
When light can make them aware
That the Path is beautiful
And the steps they take
Can be a choreography of beauty, too.

For this Path is the Beauty Way, the beautiful way,
Where all who will may Dance in Beauty
Around their own hearth fire.
What they need to light the Way
Is a lantern that is bright.
So make one.
Lit from the torch you have been given.
The eight-rayed Torch,
The Flame Within
That illuminates the Eight Directions
And the Eight Dimensions.
Make one.
Be a Sun, Grandfather.

KENNETH MEADOWS

An Instant in the Wind

To travel through that long landscape and back, back to the high mountain above the town of a thousand houses exposed to the sea and the wind. Back through that wild and empty land – *who are you? who am I ?* – without knowing what to expect, when all the instruments have been destroyed by the wind ... when nothing else remains but to continue ...

Come, he would think, breathless in the wind. The land which happened inside us no one can take from us again, not even ourselves. But God, such a long journey ahead for you and me. Not a question of imagination, but of faith.

ANDRÉ BRINK

Acknowledgements

While every effort has been made to contact the copyright holders of material used in this book, this has not always been successful. Full acknowledgement will gladly be made in future editions.

George Appleton, 'The Heart of a Child', taken from *Journey for a Soul* (Harper Collins Publishers Ltd, 1974).

Sri Aurobindo, 'Revelation', taken from *Collected Poems* (Sri Aurobindo Ashram, Publication Department, Pondicherry). Reproduced by the kind permission of the Sri Aurobindo Ashram Trust.

María Bravo Calderara, 'The People of Orpheus', taken from *Captured Voices*, edited by Fiona Whytehead and Janna Letts (Victor Gollancz, 1999). Copyright © María Bravo Calderara.

André Brink, extract from *An Instant in the Wind*, (Vintage/Ebury, a division of Random House Group Ltd, 1991). Used by the permission of Human & Rosseau, Cape Town.

Ernesto Cardenal, extract from 'The Music of the Spheres', translated by Dinah Livingstone (Katabasis, London, 1990). 'The Music of the Spheres' is one cantiga from Ernesto Cardenal's *Cántico Cósmico* (Editorial Nueva Nicaragua, Mangua, 1989).

Sheila Cassidy, extract taken from *Sharing the Darkness* (Darton, Longman and Todd Ltd). Copyright © 1988. Used by permission of the publishers.

Ch'ang Chien, 'Hermitage at Broken-Hill Monastery', taken from *A Golden Treasury of Chinese Poetry*, translated by John A. Turner (Renditions Books, Hong Kong, 1976, p. 101).

Tony Conran's translation of 'Shirt of a Lad', taken from *Welsh Verse* (Seren, 1986).

Wendy Cope, 'I Worry', taken from *Serious Concerns* (Faber & Faber, 1992).

Jeni Couzyn, 'Dawn', taken from *A Time to Be Born* (Firelizard, 1999). Thanks to Jeni Couzyn and Firelizard for permission to print this piece.

Donald Davie, 'Ordinary God', taken from *Collected Poems* (Carcanet Press Ltd).

Anthony de Mello's retelling of 'A Hasidic Tale', taken from *The Prayer of the Frog* (Gujarat Sahitya Prakash Publisher and Book-Sellers, India).

Elizabeth Jennings, 'Friendship; Identity', taken from *Collected Poems* (Carcanet Press Ltd, 1987).

Elizabeth Jennings, 'I Count the Moments', taken from *Collected Poems* (Carcanet Press Ltd, 1987).

Aung San Suu Kyi, extract taken from *Freedom from Fear and Other Writings*, edited by Michael Aris (Penguin Books, 1991). Copyright © Aung San Suu Kyi, 1991. Reproduced by permission of Penguin Books Ltd.

D. H. Lawrence, 'Song of a Man Who Has Come Through', taken from *The Complete Poems of D. H. Lawrence* (Penguin Group, UK). Used by permission of Laurence Pollinger Ltd and the Estate of Frieda Lawrence Ravagli.

Laurie Lee, 'April Rise', taken from *Selected Poems* (Penguin Books). Copyright © Laurie Lee, 1993. Reprinted by permission of Peters Fraser & Dunlop Group on behalf of the Estate of Laurie Lee.

Eiluned Lewis, 'We Who Were Born', taken from *Morning Song and Other Poems*. Used by permission of the Society of Authors on behalf of the Literary Estate of Eiluned Lewis.

Kenneth Meadows, 'The Commission Given to "Flying Horse" by Mystic Medicine Chief "Silver Bear"', taken from *The Medicine Way* (Element Books, 1990). Copyright © Kenneth Meadows.

W. S. Merwin, 'The Highway', taken from *The First Four Books of Poems* (Copper Canyon Press). Copyright © 1960 by W. S. Merwin. Reprinted by permission of Copper Canyon Press, P.O. Box 271, Port Townsend, WA 98368-0271, USA.

Norman Nicholson, 'The Burning Bush', taken from *Five Fires* (Faber & Faber).

R. A. Nicholson's translation of 'Bábá Kúhí of Shíráz', taken from *Translations of Eastern Poetry and Prose*, by R. A. Nicholson (Cambridge University Press, 1923).

Brian Patten, 'After Frost', taken from *Vanishing Trick*. Copyright © Brian Patten.

Fernando Pessoa, 'To Be Great, Be Entire', taken from *Selected Poems*, translated by Jonathan Griffin. Copyright © Assírio & Alvim, Lisbon.

Kathleen Raine, 'Seventh Day', taken from *Collected Poems* (Golgonooza Press, 2000, p. 92). Copyright © Kathleen Raine.

Anne Ridler, 'At Parting', taken from *Collected Poems* (Carcanet Press Ltd, 1997).

Vernon Scannell, 'Nettles'. Copyright © Vernon Scannell.

Grace Schulman, 'The Law', taken from *Burn Down the Icons* (Princeton University Press). Copyright © Grace Schulman. Reprinted by the permission of Grace Schulman.

David Scott, 'A Nun on the Platform', taken from *Selected Poems* (Bloodaxe Books, 1998).

Chief Seathl, 'Chief Seathl's Testament', taken from *The Great Chief Sends Word*. Distributed by One Village, Chalbury, OX7 35Q.

Vikram Seth, 'All You Who Sleep Tonight', taken from *All You Who Sleep Tonight*. Copyright © Vikram Seth 1987, 1990. First published in the UK by Faber & Faber.

Luci Shaw, 'Conversion', reprinted from *The Sighting* (Harold Shaw Publishers). Used by permission of Harold Shaw Publishers, Colorado Springs, CO 80920, USA. All rights reserved.

Stephen Spender, 'To My Daughter', taken from *Collected Poems, 1928–1985* (Faber & Faber). Copyright © 1985 Stephen Spender. Reproduced by the kind permission of the Estate of Stephen Spender.

Stephen Spender, 'The Truly Great', taken from *Collected Poems, 1928–1985* (Faber & Faber). Copyright © 1985 Stephen Spender. Reproduced by the kind permission of the Estate of Stephen Spender.

R. S. Thomas, 'In Church', taken from *Selected Poems 1946–1968* (Bloodaxe Books, 1986).

R. S. Thomas, 'Journeys', taken from *Mass for Hard Times* (Bloodaxe Books, 1992).

Trán Đúc Uyén, 'A Letter to My Future Child', translated by Huynh Sash Thong, taken from *An Anthology of Vietnamese Poems*, edited by Huynh Sash Thong (Yale University Press, 1996).

Derek Walcott, 'Map of the New World: 1 Archipelagoes', taken from *Collected Poems, 1948–1984* (Faber & Faber, 1986).

Keith Ward, extract from *God, Chance and Necessity* (Oneworld). Copyright © Keith Ward, 1996. Reproduced by permission of Oneworld Publications.

Ioanna-Veronika Warwick, 'Penelope and Odysseus as One Person'. Copyright © Ioanna-Veronika Warwick.

Anna Wickham, 'The Little Language', taken from *The Writings of Anna Wickham* (Virago Press, 1984). Copyright © George Hepburn and Margaret Hepburn.

W. B. Yeats, 'The Song of the Wandering Aengus', taken from *The Collected Poems of W. B. Yeats* (Franklin Mint Corporation, 1979). Used by the permission of A. P. Watt Ltd on behalf of Michael B. Yeats.

Yevgeny Yevtushenko, 'Colours', taken from *The Collected Poems* (Mainstream Publishing).

Danah Zohar and Ian Marshall, extract taken from *Spiritual Intelligence: The Ultimate Intelligence* (Bloomsbury, 1999).

Index of first lines, titles and authors

Index of programme titles

The poetry, prose and interviews included in this collection were featured in the following programmes of *Something Understood*:

Something Understood